Finish Line Faith

2 TIMOTHY

MATT PROCTOR

Everyday Exposition Series

OCC Press
Joplin, Missouri

In partnership with HIM Publications

This book is dedicated to the memories of my father-in-law Don Bunton and my grandfather I.O. Weede, who both passed away during its writing. Both were farmers, family men, and faithful elders who loved the Lord and encouraged me. Both finished well.

Contents

Series Introduction

The Everyday Exposition Series

Welcome! You hold in your hand a volume from the Everyday Exposition Series. This is not an accident. Since before the beginning of time, God has known this moment would come—a divine appointment, not with the author of this book, but with God. Each volume in this series walks through a Bible book (or books), and since the Lord speaks through Scripture, you should expect to hear his voice in the pages ahead. What else should you expect as you seek to understand God's Word better?

You can expect this book to be *faithful* to the text of the Bible. This volume is not a Bible commentary, at least not in the traditional sense. It won't explain every verse or get exegetically technical. (You won't need to know Hebrew or Greek.) Each author, however, is a past or present Bible college professor who "correctly handles the word of truth" (2 Tim. 2:15). These scholars believe "all Scripture is God-breathed," and our aim in the series is to carefully communicate the background and big ideas of God's Word (2 Tim. 3:16). The goal is to help you clearly hear his voice.

You should also expect this book to be *accessible* to you as a reader. First, it's a readable size. If each book of the Bible were a piece of geography to be explored, your author is more like a tour guide pointing out the highlights than an archaeologist digging up every square inch of ground. Larger books can give you a worm's-eye analysis of Scripture, but this smaller volume gives you the bird's-eye view. Second, it's written in understandable prose. While a technical Bible commentary might use specialized vocabulary that goes over people's heads, we've used bottom-shelf, everyday language. Preacher Charles Spurgeon once quipped that Jesus said "feed my sheep," not "feed my giraffes." So this college-level teaching is written in a church-friendly style.

Finally, you should expect this book to be *applicable* to you as a believer. "All Scripture is . . . useful for teaching, rebuking, correcting and training in righteousness" (2 Tim. 3:16). Or as someone put it, Scripture "tells us what's right, what's not right, how to get right, and how to stay right." The Bible was written to transform lives, so each chapter of the books in this series includes discussion questions with practical suggestions to help you apply God's truth. Our goal is not just to help you be a better Bible student, but a better Christ-follower as well.

The Everyday Exposition Series is a ministry of Ozark Christian College, a fully accredited Bible college and seminary, training men and women for Christian service. Since 1942, our motto has been "teaching the Word of Christ in the Spirit of Christ," and whether you're studying on your own or with a small group, we offer this resource with a prayer: *May "the word of Christ dwell in you richly"* (Col. 3:16, ESV).

Matt Proctor
President, Ozark Christian College

1

When You Feel
Like Giving In

2 Timothy 1:1–2

*"I have fought the good fight, I have finished
the race, I have kept the faith."*

— PAUL IN 2 TIMOTHY 4:7

Question: *If the Christian life is a race, have you ever felt like quitting?*
Every time I read 2 Timothy 4:7, I think of Big Jake. Jake was
a teammate on my high school track team. I ran long-distance; Jake
threw shot put. We called him Big Jake because he was, quite simply,
massive. He'd been shaving since second grade (or so it seemed), and
he had muscles in places where I didn't even have places.

However, Jake was not exactly the brightest candle on the cake.
Case in point: A few days before a meet, our team received an extra
entry in the mile race, and Big Jake volunteered to run. We could not
contain our surprise. Jake had never run *one* lap around the track, let
alone the four laps that make a mile. But it was his senior year, and
Jake wanted to go out in a blaze of glory.

The day came, the mile runners lined up, the gun fired, and to
our astonishment, Big Jake took off like a deer . . . or perhaps more
like a buffalo. He sprinted out around the first curve, opening a large
lead. Like a locomotive with a full head of steam, he was chugging
down the track. A blaze of glory indeed.

But something began to happen during the second lap. Big Jake started to slow. His stride was losing strength, the pack of runners began to pass him, and it quickly became apparent: Big Jake had burned all his fuel in that spectacular launch. He was running on fumes. Soon, he was dead last.

He was in a world of pain. Every muscle in Big Jake's body (and there were a lot of them) was screaming for him to quit. Halfway around the last lap, he just stopped running. With a mighty sigh, he bent over and grabbed his knees, fighting for air, and after taking a few moments to regain his balance, he walked slowly off the track. The blaze of glory had flickered out.

Big Jake never finished the race, and that day I marked down what I call the Big Jake Principle: *It's not how you start the race that matters. It's how you finish.*

A Difficult Life

If the Christian life is a race, have you ever felt like quitting? After all, the Christian life is hard.

On my desk, I have a large red button with the word "easy" on it. Maybe you remember the Staples commercials that featured this button. Anytime you have a problem, just push the "easy button," and all will be solved. Unfortunately, some Christians mistakenly think an easy button is included in the gift of salvation. One push, and God makes all our problems disappear. Hard time paying the bills? Press the easy button, and they'll be taken care of. Difficult boss? Press the easy button, and he's suddenly nicer than Mr. Rogers. Shouldn't we get an easy button as soon as we come out of the baptistery?

I teach at a Bible college, and one day a young man came into my office, sat down, and began a conversation with these words: "I had no idea. For some reason, I really thought when I became a Christian, my troubles would go away. I didn't know being a Christian would be so hard."

My guess is that you already know the Christian life is hard. You know because you've read your Bible. In John 16:33, Jesus says, "In this world you will have trouble." In Acts 14:22, Paul says, "We must go through many hardships to enter the kingdom of God."

But it's not just Scripture's clear warnings that alert you to this reality. Your own experience has likely taught you the Christian life is hard:

- You've struggled to get free of a sinful habit that won't let you go.
- You've ached through a painful conflict that tore your church in half.
- You've lost a friend because they didn't understand your new faith.
- You've prayed fervently for God to heal a parent, but no miracle came.

You know there is no easy button. Anyone who has followed Jesus for more than five minutes has experienced moments of defeat, fatigue, rejection, pain—have you ever been tempted to just stop? When you first became a Christian, still flush with gospel excitement, you envisioned your new life as a constant blaze of glory. But you're a few laps into the race now, the flame is flickering low, and you're ready to walk off the track.

If the Christian life is a race, have you ever felt like quitting?

A Dear Son

Timothy did.

Timothy was the apostle Paul's last earthly hope.

Paul penned the letter we read in 2 Timothy around AD 67. Some fifteen years before writing it, on a trip through the small town of Lystra, Paul met a young man whose spiritual maturity caught his attention. Timothy, perhaps age eighteen at the time, was spoken well of by all the brothers, and seeing his kingdom potential, Paul invited Timothy to travel with him on the rest of his missionary journey (Acts 16:2–3).

The invitation proved to be life-changing for both men. Timothy had been raised under the godly influence of his mother, Eunice, and his grandmother, Lois, but his father was not a believer and apparently not really in the picture. In Paul, Timothy found a spiritual father, and for over a decade and a half, Timothy looked to Paul as a mentor, model, wisdom figure, and hero.

In Timothy, Paul found the son he never had. In 2 Timothy 1:2, when Paul calls Timothy "my dear son," the word "dear" is actually the Greek word *agapētō*, or "beloved." You can hear the deep affection. While Paul taught Timothy as a rabbi would a disciple, Timothy was more than just another student. What began as a teacher/pupil relationship grew into a deep friendship. In 2 Timothy 1:4, Paul writes, "I long to see you so that I may be filled with joy." Throughout his New Testament letters, Paul mentions Timothy eighteen times by name, and in Philippians 2:20, he even says, "I have no one else like him."

Indeed, Paul entrusted to Timothy his most significant kingdom assignment—leading the church in Ephesus. Outside of Rome, Ephesus was the most strategic city in the Empire. As the capital of the Roman province of Asia Minor, it stood at a major trade crossroads, at the midpoint of both the north-south and east-west travel routes across the Empire.

Large, diverse, and affluent, Ephesus was where Paul spent his longest recorded ministry. For three years, the apostle worked "night and day" to start and establish a healthy church in this premiere city, and when he left, he didn't think he would ever return (Acts 20:25, 31).

But now, years later, came disturbing news. The congregation in Ephesus was in trouble. Along with the problems of materialism (1 Tim. 6:5–10) and divisive attitudes (1 Tim. 2:8), false teaching was threatening the church. These teachers, like wolves in sheepskin, were infiltrating the flock and leading many astray (1 Tim. 1:19–20; 4:1–3; 2 Tim. 2:17–18; 3:1–9; 4:3–4).

A Difficult Assignment

Paul and Timothy returned to Ephesus to straighten out this mess, but after hearing of a pressing need in Macedonia, Paul decided to move on, leaving Timothy behind to set matters right (1 Tim. 1:3). Now Timothy was alone with a big job on his hands. Forming a new church is hard work, but *reforming* an established church is even harder. Giving correction is always harder than giving direction.

To make matters worse, my guess is that Timothy felt like he was stepping up to the plate with three strikes already against him. First, he was young. He was in his early thirties, and the folks in the Ephesian church saw him as just another Bible college kid, still wet behind the ears. In 1 Timothy 4:12, Paul hints that some are looking down on his youth. *Strike one.*

Second, he was sickly. If you've ever been on a trip in the developing world, what do you always hear? "Don't drink the water." Apparently, no one mentioned this to Timothy, so in 1 Timothy 5:23, Paul tells him, "Stop drinking only water," citing his "stomach and . . . frequent illnesses." Can you imagine: poor Timothy is preaching a sermon when he suddenly experiences an Imodium A-D moment! His weak constitution presented many challenges to fulfilling his ministry. *Strike two.*

To top it off, Timothy was something of an introvert. He was more inclined to stand on the sidelines than to get out on the field. In just four short chapters, Paul uses thirty-five imperatives in 2 Timothy. In his two letters, Paul tells Timothy: "Do not neglect your gift . . . fight the good fight . . . fan into flame the gift of God, which is in you." Paul sounds like a coach giving a pep talk to a reluctant player. One scholar called this soft-spoken young man "timid Timothy."[1] The thought of confronting misguided leaders would have made him cringe.

That's strike three, and Timothy wants outta there. He's ready to be done with this ministry, walk off the track, and never come back. If the Christian life is a race, he feels like quitting.

A Determined Leader

So the apostle Paul picks up his pen.

Ephesus was too strategic, the false teaching too dangerous, Timothy's mission too important to let this situation go unaddressed.

It's important to add that Paul is especially urgent because he is writing this letter from prison. You might be thinking, *Paul was, like, always in prison.* Yes! Paul was what we would call a "repeat offender." Because of his bold preaching, Paul had compiled quite an arrest record, often spending time in the local lockup.

But this time was different: Paul knew this was his last imprisonment. In just a few short months—or weeks—he would face execution. In 2 Timothy 4:6, Paul writes, "I am already being poured out like a drink offering, and the time for my departure is near."

It appears that all of Paul's church planting in Asia Minor had been for naught. Nero was emperor at the time, and Christians were his favorite scapegoat. Persecution loomed on the horizon. There was no "easy button," and consequently, 2 Timothy 1:15 describes an overwhelming exodus from the churches that Paul planted. Paul writes: "You know that everyone in the province of Asia has deserted me, including Phygelus and Hermogenes."

And they weren't the last to fall away.

The book *Finishing Strong* tells the story of John Bisagno, the long-time pastor of First Baptist Church in Houston:

> When John was just about to finish college, he was having dinner at his fiancée's house one night. After supper, he was talking with his future father-in-law, Dr. Paul Beck, out on the porch. Dr. Beck had been in ministry for years.
>
> "John, as you get ready to enter the ministry, I want to give you some advice," Dr. Beck told the younger man. "Stay true to Jesus! Make sure that you keep your heart close to Jesus every day. It's a long way from here to where you're going to go, and Satan's in no hurry to get you."
>
> The older man continued, "It has been my observation that just one out of ten who start out in full-time service for the Lord at [age] twenty-one are still on track by the age of sixty-five. They're

shot down morally, they're shot down with discouragement, they're shot down with liberal theology, they get obsessed with making money . . . but for one reason or another nine out of ten fall out."

The twenty-year-old Bisagno was shocked.

"I just can't believe that!" he said. "That's impossible! That just can't be true."

Bisagno told how he went home, took one of those blank pages in the back of his Scofield Reference Bible, and wrote down the names of twenty-four young men who were his peers. These were young men in their twenties who were sold out for Jesus Christ. They were trained for ministry and burning in their desire to be used by the Lord. Bisagno relates the following with a sigh: "I am now fifty-three years old. From time to time as the years have gone by, I've had to turn back to that page in my Bible and cross out a name. I wrote down those twenty-four names when I was just twenty years of age. Thirty-three years later, there are only *three names* remaining of the original twenty-four."[2]

I don't know how many names the apostle Paul had written in the back of his Bible, but he had just crossed out Phygelus and Hermogenes (1:15). Now there was only one name left: Timothy. All the other leaders Paul was depending on had abandoned the cause.

Now, here he was, depending on this sickly, introverted young man—the apprentice he had poured his love and life into. The torch of the gospel must be passed unquenched from one generation to the next, and Paul was determined that Timothy not fumble it. He needed Timothy to be the "one out of ten" to finish well.

A Divine Encouragement

So Paul picks up his pen and writes 2 Timothy, the last known letter from the apostle's hand. In this letter to Timothy, Paul issues essentially one charge: *Don't quit!* Be faithful. Persevere. Endure. Don't give up. Don't give in. Keep running. Finish strong, Timothy! Stay on the track.

Paul is forging in Timothy what I call "finish-line faith."

This letter is a powerful tool for shaping that kind of resilient faith. This priceless gift from the aging apostle is better than any easy button. Rather than simply removing hardship, these ancient pages provide the wisdom needed to overcome hardship. The words shoot adrenaline through Timothy's weary soul.

> These ancient pages provide the wisdom needed to overcome hardship.

In fact, as we begin our study of 2 Timothy, can I tell you the end of the story? The church historian Eusebius tells us that Timothy faithfully led the church in Ephesus for the next thirty years. In AD 97, after protesting the pagan festivities surrounding the worship of the Greek goddess Artemis, he was stoned to death.

In other words, Timothy finished strong. Paul's letter had done its work.

As you study 2 Timothy, you'll find new hope surging through your soul as well. When you feel like quitting the Christian life, this letter will bring spiritual strength.

It will equip you with finish-line faith.

How?

In the course of the four chapters of 2 Timothy, Paul gives instructions on how to go on when you feel like giving in—things like remembering your heritage, meditating on the gospel, nourishing yourself on Scripture, and cultivating real community. You'll find his words to be straightforward, practical, and Spirit-inspired. They are exactly the divine encouragement a discouraged disciple needs.

In the next chapter, we'll begin our paragraph-by-paragraph study of 2 Timothy. I encourage you to review each paragraph in the Scriptures before you read the corresponding chapter in this book. God's Word is so powerful! In fact, as we close this chapter, read again Paul's first words to young Timothy. In 2 Timothy 1:2, he writes, "Grace, mercy and peace from God the Father and Christ Jesus our Lord."

I know of a woman who decided to pray for a different friend each day for a year. Each morning, she would write out her prayer on a postcard and send it, allowing that day's friend to "eavesdrop" on her prayer closet as she prayed for them. What an encouragement to listen in as one of God's saints intercedes on your behalf!

That's exactly what Paul is doing here for Timothy. Before the apostle moves into the body of his letter, he pauses to let Timothy overhear his prayers on Timothy's behalf. What does Paul pray for this disheartened young man? He asks God to bestow three of his richest blessings: grace, mercy, and peace.

Don't miss the powerful message here. That's a mighty prayer:

- Grace: God's worth to the worthless
- Mercy: God's help to the helpless
- Peace: God's rest to the restless[3]

As Timothy eavesdropped on Paul's prayer closet, hearing him ask God for these blessings, the young man drew great strength.

Here's the good news: These blessings are available to you too. God still gives his grace, mercy, and peace to those who ask, and it is still God our Father who enables his children to endure whatever hardships come our way.

What a simple but essential truth for us as we begin this book: *God* gives us the strength to finish the race. While each chapter will suggest a way to go on when you feel like giving in, these suggestions are simply means of accessing the Father's resources. It is God—and God alone—who will bring us safely home. The missionary Hudson Taylor said, "It is not by trying to be faithful, but in looking to the Faithful One, that we win the victory."[4]

> God gives us the strength to finish the race.

The prophet Isaiah put it this way, "Those who wait for the LORD will gain new strength; they will mount up with wings like eagles, they will run and not get tired" (Isaiah 40:31, NASB).

With God's help, you can be the "one out of ten" who finishes well. Keep reading and let him forge in you a finish-line faith. Remember the Big Jake Principle: *It's not how you start the race that matters. It's how you finish.*

Discussion Questions

1. What is something in your life you didn't finish but now wish you had?
2. Think back to when you first trusted Christ. Did you expect the Christian life to be hard or easy? How would you describe it now?
3. If the Christian life is a race, have you ever felt like quitting? What or who helped you navigate that struggle?
4. What are the consequences of quitting? What are the rewards of finishing well?
5. Which of the three spiritual blessings—grace, mercy, and peace—do you think you need the most?

TAKE ACTION Take time to ask God for the spiritual blessing you most desire.

2

Remember Your Heritage

2 Timothy 1:3–5

"What you have as heritage, take now as task; for thus you will make it your own."

— JOHANN WOLFGANG VON GOETHE

July 1, 1898. Cuba. The Spanish-American War. At the bottom of San Juan Hill, Lt. Colonel Teddy Roosevelt prepared to lead the charge against 750 Spanish soldiers ordered to hold the heights. Just weeks before, he had resigned his civilian naval commission to join the cavalry, saying, "I want to explain to my children someday why I did take part in the war, not why I didn't." So that July morning, Lt. Colonel Roosevelt strapped on his boots and led his Rough Riders regiment up the hill under fierce Spanish gunfire and on to victory. For his courage, he was awarded the Congressional Medal of Honor.

June 6, 1944. Normandy, France. World War II. Sitting in the troop transport ships, Brigadier General Teddy Roosevelt Jr. prepared to lead the attack on the most heavily fortified coast in history. Surely he was thinking of his father. President Roosevelt had poured his life into his four sons—telling them stories, teaching them horseback riding and how to handle a gun. When the Japanese ambassador visited the White House, President Roosevelt said, "Bring your sumo champions with you. I want my boys to learn how to wrestle." They wrestled in the living room of the White House! He instilled in his boys patriotism, duty, and a willingness to lead.

That's why Teddy Roosevelt Jr. was now preparing to lead the D-Day invasion. At first, his superiors had denied his request to go: "You're fifty-seven years old. No other general is going ashore with the first wave of troops." But he insisted, "It will steady the men to know I'm with them." After his third request, they finally agreed. So that June morning, Teddy Jr. strapped on his boots and led the charge up the beach under fierce German gunfire and on to victory. For his courage, he was awarded the Congressional Medal of Honor . . . just like his father.

The leadership of each generation is the legacy they leave to the next.

When my wife, Katie, and I were preparing to celebrate ten years of marriage, we pulled out our wedding video to watch it with our children. If you saw our wedding video, you would be amazed at how slim and handsome I once was! My kids were certainly surprised. As she watched our exchange of vows, my five-year-old, Lydia, turned to me: "Daddy, you sure do look different there." Seven-year-old Luke replied matter-of-factly, "That's because he was young back then."

Luke was right. I was young. Twenty-one years old and immature, I didn't know the first thing about how to live well with another person, how to love my wife "as Christ loved the church" (Eph. 5:25). Ask Katie, and she'll tell you: that first year of marriage was hard. Tension, discouragement, conflict. As I watched the video, I thought, *What kept us going that year? How in the world did we make it?*

In the video, you can see Katie's Grandpa and Grandma Bunton. We were married on their sixty-fifth wedding anniversary. You can see both sets of my grandparents—each married for over fifty years. On the screen are Katie's parents, at that point married forty-one years, and my parents with twenty-three years of marriage.

That's how we made it: we had received a heritage of faithfulness. All those couples experienced hard times, but they worked their way through to the other side. We knew we could do no less.

The leadership of each generation is the legacy we will leave to the next.

The Power of Remembering

Young Timothy wasn't sure he was going to make it. Overwhelmed and underappreciated in his ministry in Ephesus, Timothy felt like giving up. He was under fierce enemy fire and wondering, *Where will I find the courage to lead the charge?* In the opening paragraph of 2 Timothy, Paul answers that question: remember your heritage.

As Paul forges in Timothy a finish-line faith, he points the discouraged disciple backward. Three times in 1:3–5, he speaks of remembering. Specifically, he stirs in Timothy the remembrance of his heritage. Paul begins by mentioning his own heritage: "I serve, as my ancestors did" (1:3). He then goes on to mention Timothy's heritage: "I am reminded of your sincere faith, which first lived in your grandmother Lois and in your mother Eunice and, I am persuaded, now lives in you also" (1:5).

Paul's message here is, "I am following in the footsteps of those who've gone before me. Now you follow in the footsteps of those who've gone before you."

Surely the names in verse five evoked powerful memories for Timothy of his childhood years. We know that Timothy's father was Greek and not a believer, but his grandmother and mother were Jewish. Likely, Lois, Eunice, and Timothy all became Christians under Paul's preaching in Lystra on his first missionary journey (Acts 14:6–7). However, even before placing their faith in Christ, these two godly women taught the boy Timothy their Jewish Scriptures, what we now call the Old Testament. In 2 Timothy 3:15, Paul says, "from infancy you have known the Holy Scriptures."

What images flooded Timothy's memory? Did he remember seeing his grandmother praying on her knees every morning as the sun rose? Did he think back to the times when his little heart pounded as his mother told bedtime stories of the Hebrew heroes of faith—Abraham, Joseph, Moses, David?

One thing is clear: Paul wants Timothy to feel a strong sense of responsibility to preserve the godly heritage he has received—to feel it deep in his DNA. His grandmother and mother had remained faithful; he can do no less. He must keep the faith alive. He can't quit the race because he has a baton to carry, a story to continue, an honor to uphold.

The leadership of each generation is the legacy they leave to the next.

> The leadership of each generation is the legacy they leave to the next.

When you feel discouraged and your pace is slowing, a backward look may help inspire forward motion. Recalling the examples of those who've gone before you can:

- *Provide wisdom.* Their lives may show you what your guiding values look like when they're fleshed out. Their decisions can help shape yours.
- *Deepen your sense of identity.* Only when you know whom you came from can you know who you are. Even windshields come with rearview mirrors.
- *Give you hope.* When you remember others who've persevered through trials to come out stronger, you begin to believe your own difficulties may not be fatal after all.
- *Inspire faithfulness.* Their lives were in some way an investment in yours. You want your life to provide a healthy return on their investment.

Your Biblical Heritage

But what exactly are the remembrances that firm up a faltering faith? What kind of heritage are we to remember? One type of heritage Paul references here is biblical. The apostle saw himself standing in the long line of his Old Testament "forefathers," following God the way Noah and Joshua and Daniel had centuries before. From this, he drew strength.

The writer of Hebrews lived with similar wisdom. Writing to Jewish Christians who were considering discarding their faith, the author points them back to their biblical heritage in Hebrews 11.

Rudy is still one of my favorite movies. It's the true story of Daniel "Rudy" Ruettiger, who grew up dreaming of playing football for Notre Dame. Everyone tells him it's impossible, but his heart and hard work eventually get him into Notre Dame, where he makes the football team as a walk-on, plays for two downs in the last game of his senior year, and officially enters the annals of Notre Dame football.

Halfway through the movie, Rudy enters the Notre Dame locker room for the first time. For him, this is holy ground. He starts to move slowly through the darkened room, locker to locker, and in hushed tones, he begins to list Notre Dame's football history: "The Four Horsemen. Knute Rockne. Moose Krause. Angelo Bertelli. Johnny Lujack. Paul Hornung could've dressed in this locker." When the going got tough for Daniel Ruettiger, that rich heritage kept him going. He knew the story of Notre Dame football, and he wanted to be a small part of that great story.

In Hebrews 11, the author takes his readers through the darkened locker room of faith. As he moves from locker to locker, in hushed tones he tells the amazing stories of those who, against all odds, kept on trusting God. It is their message of faithful endurance, echoing through the years, that the Hebrews writer wants his readers to hear. He follows Hebrews 11 with this charge: "Therefore, since we are surrounded by such a great cloud of witnesses . . . let us run with perseverance the race marked out for us" (Heb. 12:1).

This message is for us today as well. This "great cloud of witnesses"—those are *your* spiritual ancestors. As a Christian, *you* are an heir of Abraham. As the church, *you* are the new Israel. Those names in Hebrews 11 are your spiritual genealogy, and their faith courses through your veins. Their story is now your story, which means you can't quit. When you feel like giving up, reflect on your biblical heritage. Find a character from Scripture who resonates with you and meditate on their life. Of course, the greatest example in Scripture

> Their story is now your story, which means you can't quit.

is Christ: ". . . fixing our eyes on Jesus, the pioneer and perfecter of our faith. For the joy set before him he endured the cross, scorning its shame, and sat down at the right hand of the throne of God. Consider him who endured such opposition from sinners, so that you will not grow weary and lose heart" (Heb. 12:2–3).

Your Historical Heritage

Beyond the last page of Scripture, you will also find strength in the pages of church history—the stories of great saints through the ages. Perhaps you've never read the story of the aged Polycarp, a second-century martyr who was given one last chance to recant his faith before being burned at the stake. His reply: "Eighty and six years have I served him, and he never once wronged me; how then can I blaspheme my King who saved me?"

Or the story of William Tyndale, who labored tirelessly to put into people's hands a Bible they could read in their own language. He eventually printed the first English New Testament, despite the Catholic Church's threats to execute anyone owning a non-Latin Bible. After suffering a shipwreck, loss of manuscripts, exile, pursuit by secret agents, and betrayal by a friend, William was captured and strangled, and his dead body was burned at the stake. (How can I ever take lightly this English Bible I hold in my hand?)

Throughout history, the lives of the great men and women of God—Amy Carmichael, David Brainerd, Susanna Wesley, Jim Elliot, George Müller—move me (if you don't know who they are, each is worth at least a Google search). They remind me that I am not an island. I am part of a vast continent called the kingdom of God, and it stretches back through the centuries and around the globe. We are part of a bigger story, and those who have walked before us inspire us.

Listen to my friend J. K. Jones tell his own story:

> There was a season in the whirlwind of books, seminary, and ministry where I believed I could not go on. Criticism, overwork, and little rest took its toll. One Sunday night, after evening worship and a difficult meeting, I thought I was coming apart. I wondered

if this was what it was like when a person had a "breakdown." I cried and couldn't stop. My wife took me and our family over to the home of dear friends. . . . Those precious people reached into their pockets and gave us all the cash they had . . . and offered these wise words, "Get out of the area code and let us know where you are." We loaded the car and drove all night, spending the next couple of weeks in Arkansas with my wife's parents.

I didn't think I wanted to go back to that ministry or to that church. My soul was dry, my mind dull, and my heart broken. My mother-in-law knew better than I did what was happening and what was at stake. For several days I said very little and mostly slept. One morning I heard a knock at the door of the bedroom. I didn't answer. The door creaked open, and Mom Graham threw me a Snickers candy bar and a book. The only word from her mouth was, "Enjoy."

I did not open either gift for a while, but slowly I began to eat the candy bar and then turned my appetite to the book. Mom had found an old copy of *The Biography of David Livingstone*.[1] I devoured it, reading and rereading words, sentences, and paragraphs. Livingstone's life of courage, endurance, and character spoke deeply to my soul. It was as if God himself spoke loudly and firmly to me through that book, "If Livingstone can persevere, so can you." After some more days of rest, we returned, and our most productive years of ministry in that church followed.[2]

May I challenge you to read the lives of faithful Christians through the ages? Tim Hansel writes, "Theology must always become biography," and when I see the truth of God fleshed out in the lives of people, it challenges me to do likewise.[3]

Your Personal Heritage

Not only can the history of the universal church spur you to go the distance, so can the history of your church—the group of believers you worship with has a history as well. Do you know that story? Talk to the older members of the church; ask them questions about the good times and hard times.

If you are one of the "grayheads," be intentional about telling those stories—not to compare or complain, but to capture the characteristics that define your congregation. Like tribal elders, seize the moments "around the campfire" to pass on the history of your people to the next generation of young warriors. These stories can embed your congregation's historic commitment to excellence—or evangelistic heart, or sacrificial generosity, or risky faith—deep in the next generation's imagination.

In addition to your church family, your biological family may also have given you a spiritual legacy. I heard about a mother explaining proudly to her daughter that her grandfather was a preacher, her great-great-grandfather was a preacher, and her great-great-great grandfather was a preacher. The little girl replied, "Wow! We sure come from a long line of grandfathers."

Maybe you come from a long line of believers. It's been said that God has children, but no grandchildren, and it's true that no one gets into the kingdom on the coattails of their parents. You can't inherit your family's faith; however, you can certainly catch it. An authentic Christian example is contagious, and perhaps it was the witness of your mother or father, aunt or grandfather that brought you to Christ.

Maybe you didn't grow up with a Christian family, but you had a spiritual mentor of some kind. Someone told you and taught you about Jesus. While Timothy had a believing grandmother and mother, it was a mentor, Paul, who discipled him in Christ. Notice how Paul highlights their personal relationship in our 2 Timothy text: "Recalling your tears, I long to see you, so that I may be filled with joy" (1:4). The apostle is reminding Timothy of his love for him and of his past investment in Timothy's life (1:6). Perhaps you have a "Paul" who has poured into your life.

The point is this: think about your own personal heritage. When I'm having a hard day in ministry, I look up at the signatures on the "Certificate of Ordination" that hangs on my wall, the men who laid hands on me to set me apart for ministry:

- My dad—a corporate executive, elder, and the most servant-hearted man I know.
- My longtime hometown preacher—who recruited me to ministry and closed his sermons for thirty years with the words, "Remember: God loves you, Jesus loves you, and I love you." Somehow I knew he meant it.
- My father-in-law—a big, quiet farmer and church elder who passed away during the writing of this book. The line of people at his visitation lasted almost four hours. Generous and faithful, he cast a long shadow with his life.
- My grandfather—another elder and farmer. (Ironically his last name was Weede!) He only finished eighth grade, but for years, he was a diligent Bible student and teacher. He too went to be with the Lord during the writing of this book. He literally prayed for me by name every day from the day I was born until the day he died.

When I see those names, I realize: *I can't quit.*

Who's on your list of names? Someone invested in you. Whose faith "now lives in you" (1:5)? I have a student who keeps in the back of his Bible the pictures of those whose lives pointed him to God: a parent, a nineteenth-century missionary, a minister. Whose pictures would be in the back of your Bible?

When you're tired and feel like giving in, hear Paul's message to Timothy: remember your heritage and keep going. A backward look can inspire forward motion.

By the way, don't forget: your example can shape those who come after you. Your picture may someday be in the back of someone else's Bible.

The leadership of your generation is the legacy you'll leave to the next.

Discussion Questions

1. What is your family's spiritual heritage?
2. Whom in the Bible do you relate to the most?
3. What can you learn from the heroes of the faith from church history?
4. What names would be on a list of the people who have invested in you?
5. How have they helped you run your race?

TAKE ACTION Send a note of thanks to someone on your list of people who have invested into you.

3

Rely on the Spirit

2 Timothy 1:6–7

"Christian sermons ought to ask more of people than mortals can rightfully do . . . because we are equipped with inward supernatural potency, thanks to the Holy Spirit. Christians have in the Holy Spirit more power than they know what to do with."

— LEE ECLOV

Growing up, I dreamed of being Superman.

As a child, I was profoundly unheroic: a quiet, skinny kid with pencil-thin arms and a paper-thin chest. I had little athletic ability, wore glasses, and was a total bookworm. When I disobeyed my parents, they grounded me for a week . . . *from reading!* Can you get any nerdier than that? I felt like an eight-year-old Clark Kent—awkward, fumbling, and powerless.

But when Christopher Reeve's *Superman* swooped into theaters, my eight-year-old imagination was captured. I wanted to fly, bend steel with my bare hands, and feel bullets bounce off my chest, and I wanted pectorals big enough to handle that giant red *S*. At eight, my chest could only accommodate skinny letters, like a lowercase *l* or *i*.[1] Most of all, I longed to have supernatural power coursing through my body—the ability to manage any mayhem life threw my way.

Timothy could identify. I don't know if he had a skinny chest, but Timothy had a weak stomach, hesitant voice, and faint heart. Staring into the teeth of a challenging church, he felt like Clark

Kent—powerless. The bad guys in Ephesus were not imaginary (see 2 Tim. 3:1–9). They were potent adversaries, and Timothy wondered: *Where will I find the strength to deal with these difficulties?*

Ever asked that question? Maybe you're facing a formidable foe—cancer, conflict, a dark temptation—and wondering how you will handle it. You are painfully aware of your own limitations, and as you size up the situation, you know your resources—physical, emotional, intellectual—are simply not enough.

Where can you find superpowers when you really need them?

In 2 Timothy 1:6–7, Paul gives the answer.

Who Is the Holy Spirit?

Before we go any further, we need to set up a theological context, because the Holy Spirit can be a mysterious figure. You may recognize his picture in the Bible when you see it—a wind, a fire, a dove—but you may not know much about him. Briefly, what does the Bible teach about the Holy Spirit?

First, the Holy Spirit is *a personal being.* Some mistakenly picture him as simply an impersonal force. As one misguided teacher put it, "The Holy Spirit is not a person, but the power God the Father uses—much as a man uses electricity."[2] That couldn't be further from the truth. Rather, he is a person with consciousness, personality, and a will (Acts 13:2; 15:28). In fact, in places like John 16:13–14, the masculine personal pronoun "he" is used in reference to the Spirit. After a trip to the barber, I don't want my kids to say, "Oh look, *it* got a new haircut." I am not a thing, but a person, and so is the Holy Spirit. Call him "he."

Second, the Holy Spirit is *a divine being.* Unfortunately, he is sometimes treated like the junior member of the Trinity, the kid brother of the Godhead—no respect. However, the Bible teaches his full equality with the Father and Son, divine in every sense that they are. He is eternal (Heb. 9:14), omnipresent (Ps. 139:7–10), knows everything God the Father knows (1 Cor. 2:10–11), and helped create the world (Gen 1:2; Ps. 104:30). In Matthew 28:19, the disciples are commanded to baptize "in the name of the Father and of the Son and of the Holy Spirit," placing the Spirit at the same level as the first two.

Third, for the believer, the Holy Spirit is *an indwelling being*. I heard a preacher say once that the Father is God *without* skin, Jesus is God *with* skin, and the Holy Spirit is God *within my* skin. When we are baptized by faith into Christ, the Spirit comes to live within us (Acts 2:38). The Holy Ghost becomes our Holy Guest. In the Old Testament, God promised to be *with* his people, but in the New Testament, God promises to be *in* his people. What a difference a preposition makes!

As a Christian, I am called to imitate Christ, but on my own, I can no more live like Jesus than I can play basketball like Michael Jordan. But what if the spirit of Michael Jordan could somehow inhabit my body and play basketball through me? (Yes, I'm describing the movie *Like Mike*.) My performance wouldn't be perfect, but it would be more than I could ever achieve on my own. Likewise, while I can't imitate Christ in my own strength, his Spirit can live through me. I'll never look exactly like him, but I'll start to look more and more like him because he's not just with me, but *in* me.

It's this transforming truth that Paul emphasizes for Timothy. Look at 2 Timothy 1:6, 7, 8, 14, and 2:1. In each verse, he references God's power that is available to us—no, *in* us. The message is clear: you may feel like Clark Kent, but through the Holy Spirit, supernatural abilities can be yours.

The Supernatural Ability to Serve

In 2 Timothy 1:6, Paul challenges Timothy to "fan into flame the gift of God, which is in you through the laying on of my hands." Paul seems to be reminding Timothy of his "ordination service," when a group of elders and the apostle himself laid hands on him, spoke words of exhortation, and imparted a spiritual gift to him (1 Tim. 4:14). This is one way the Holy Spirit empowers the believer: the endowment of spiritual gifts.

A spiritual gift is a supernatural ability that equips a believer for service to God's people. In some cases, the Spirit simply supernaturally enhances a natural ability someone already has and directs it toward kingdom use. (Of course, the natural ability was originally from God as well.) A capable leader in the business world, upon coming to Christ, may become a gifted leader in the church.

In other cases, the ability is completely new to the believer. A high school speech teacher once told my friend Stacy his class presentation was so bad that he should never speak in public again. (This teacher clearly did not have the gift of encouragement.) But when Stacy became a Christian at age nineteen, he believed God had called him to preach and, thanks to the Spirit's gifting, became a very effective proclaimer of God's Word.

If we read through the major New Testament texts on spiritual gifts (1 Cor. 12:1–31; Rom. 12:4–8; Eph. 4:7–16; 1 Pet. 4:10–11), two truths would stand out:

1. Every believer has a gift. You may think, *When God was handing out gifts, he must've missed me.* But last time I checked, God doesn't make spare people whom he's not planning to use. Some may have a greater number of gifts (like the five-talents servant in Matthew 25:14–30), but everybody has at least one ability to use in service (see 1 Cor. 12:7; 12:11; and 1 Pet. 4:10). If you have the Spirit, you have a spiritual gift.

2. Spiritual gifts come in all shapes and sizes. We can often focus on one or two gifts that are prominent, like preaching or leadership. But even a quick read through the above passages will show that *all* Spirit-given abilities are necessary for building up the church—mercy, encouragement, giving, and more. A gift that is more "behind-the-scenes" is no less important than those that are "up front."

We don't know what gift the Spirit had bestowed on Timothy, but whatever it was, Timothy apparently had considered shelving it. In 1 Timothy 4:14, Paul says, "Do not neglect your gift," or as The Message translates it, "that special gift of ministry you were given . . . keep that dusted off and in use." Again, in 2 Timothy 1:6,

Paul urges this young pastor to keep his gift ready to go. The Spirit had empowered him for ministry, and to keep that ministry gift under wraps would be like Superman refusing to use his powers to help other people.

May I do some "urging" with you? Spiritual gifts are wonderful grace-presents from God to the church, but they carry with them a few inherent dangers. Heed these warnings about spiritual gifts:

- *Don't use them as a cop-out for radical service.* When the toilet is overflowing in the church bathroom, don't walk by with the "sorry I can't help because my gift is evangelism" excuse. Grab a plunger. We're all called to serve, even if it's not always in our giftedness "sweet spot."
- *Don't use them as a substitute for spiritual maturity.* The gifts of the Spirit cannot take the place of the fruit of the Spirit (Gal. 5:22–23). I've met a few Christians who acted like their special gifts—preaching, music, etc.—exempted them from virtues like humility and patience. Read Paul's first letter to the gifted-but-immature church in Corinth: a certain competence does not make Christlike character optional.
- *Don't misuse them out of pride.* We might be tempted to use our abilities to gain personal recognition, but spiritual gifts are for the building of God's kingdom, not our own. First Peter 4:10 says they are to be used "to serve others," and 1 Corinthians 12:7 says gifts are "given for the common good."
- *Don't "unuse" them out of laziness or fear.* The church needs all hands on deck. Author Leslie Flynn notes: "Practice of the biblical doctrine of gifts taps reservoirs of godly manpower, thaws out frozen assets, roots out unemployment among saints, reflects the universal priesthood of believers, and edifies the church."[3] Discover your gifts by examining your life, trying different kinds of service opportunities, and asking for others' input on what you do best. Once you find your spiritual strong suit, make the most of it. Christianity is not a spectator sport.

As a friend of mine says, "You got into the ministry when you got out of the baptistery." Use your gift.

The Supernatural Ability to Endure

The Holy Spirit gives us not only the ability to serve but also the ability to endure. He is the one who forges in us a finish-line faith. No matter what you face, Paul says, the indwelling presence of God is enough to sustain you. I saw a church sign that read, "The problem before us is never as great as the power within us."

> The indwelling presence of God is enough to sustain you.

And make no mistake: there certainly will be problems. In 2 Timothy 1:7, Paul says, "For the Spirit God gave us does not make us timid, but gives us power, love and self-discipline." In ancient times, the Greek word for "timid" was sometimes used to indicate "cowardice in battle," and Timothy would fight battles on many fronts. Manipulative false teachers, wayward church members, loneliness, physical fatigue, the temptations that usually plague a young single man in a sexually charged culture—all of these would war against his soul. But Paul reminds Timothy of the spiritual resources the Holy Spirit will provide. Specifically, he mentions three: the *power to endure difficult circumstances*, the *love to endure difficult people*, and the *self-discipline to endure difficult temptations*.

1. *Power to Endure Difficult Circumstances.* The first Spirit-resource Paul mentions in 2 Timothy 1:7 is power. The Greek word here is *dunamis*, from which we form our English word "dynamite." Paul's constant prayer for God's people was that "out of his glorious riches he may strengthen you with power through his Spirit in your inner being" (Eph. 3:16). New Testament scholar William Barclay notes that this *dunamis* is "the power to shoulder the back-breaking task, the power to stand erect in face of the shattering situation, the power to retain faith in face of the soul-searing sorrow and the wounding disappointment."[4]

I heard a preacher once tell the story of a float in the Rose Parade that suddenly came to a stop. It had run out of gas, backing up the entire procession. The irony: the float represented the Standard Oil company! They had failed to tap the vast reservoirs of fuel at their disposal. Too often, we as Christians try to tackle life's challenges in our own strength, without tapping the vast and available power of God. As Christian journalist Andrée Seu Peterson confesses, "I've whined so much about a poor memory, depression, and insomnia that a friend suggested I take a bottle of 'white out' and delete Philippians 4:13 since I wasn't using it anyway."[5]

How do we access the Spirit's power? Quite simply, by faith. Will you trust God to do "immeasurably more than all we ask or imagine, according to his power that is at work within us" (Eph. 3:20)? Will you refuse to see as hyperbole, "Everything is possible for one who believes" (Mark 9:23)? Will you expect to be "strengthened with all power according to his glorious might so that you may have great endurance and patience" (Col. 1:11)? For those believers who do these things, they will, as Peterson writes, "look at the size of their problems and then look at the size of Resurrection power and decide there's no contest."[6]

Richard Wurmbrand experienced that power. Wurmbrand was the founder of the Voice of the Martyrs ministry. As a pastor in Romania behind the Iron Curtain, he was arrested in 1948 and tortured for fourteen years because of his faith in Christ. In his book, *Tortured for Christ*, he wrote,

> It was strictly forbidden to preach to other prisoners . . . . It was understood that whoever was caught doing this received a severe beating. But a number of us decided to pay the price for the privilege of preaching, so we accepted their terms. It was a deal: we preached, and they beat us. We were happy preaching; they were happy beating us—so everyone was happy.[7]

Listen: this kind of power is simply not natural. Normal people do not endure circumstances that difficult and call themselves "happy." Your average Clark Kent couldn't take it. The power to endure in this way must be a power from somewhere outside this world—a power from heaven. Mind you, this supernatural power that courses through our veins doesn't mean we are free from pain. Bullets didn't bounce off Jesus' chest. When life wounds us, we will still bleed. But this supernatural power does mean we can come through crises to finish strong.

2. *Love to Endure Difficult People.* The second Spirit-resource Paul lists in 2 Timothy 1:7 is love. The Greek word here is *agape,* which someone once defined as "an unconditional commitment to an imperfect person." Timothy surely faced some imperfect people in Ephesus—folks with bad attitudes, immature thinking, unwise habits, and needy personalities.

Welcome to the church.

Every congregation has difficult people. I once heard someone say, "If you want to be the light of the world, you're going to attract a few bugs." My hunch is that there are a few folks in your church who bug you. Or maybe they're outside the church—a boss, a neighbor, or a family member who frustrates you, perhaps even antagonizes you. At best, they drive you to impatience. At worst, they stir up feelings of anger, bitterness, and even hatred.

How will we ever learn to *love* such people? Only by the Spirit's work in our lives. Remember that love is first in the list of the fruit of the Spirit, and as we listen to his promptings in our life, we will learn to seek the best for the difficult people we encounter. He will guide our actions toward them, and eventually our hearts will follow.

During my junior year in Bible college, I was convinced the two freshmen in the dorm room next to mine were not going to heaven. They stayed up late, slept through classes, played their rock music loudly, and proudly displayed their support for the Los Angeles Lakers.

Clearly, they were pagans.

One night, as I was studying, they turned up their music, and I reached my breaking point. I stormed next door and vented my righteous indignation. Someone once said that when you're angry, you'll give the best speech you'll ever regret—and that night I gave those guys a really good speech.

When I returned to my room to resume studying and began to calm down, I could hear the Holy Spirit's convicting whisper: "Go apologize." I didn't *want* to go apologize, so for the next hour, I wrestled with the Holy Spirit. "They deserved it," I argued. "They need someone to offer correction. I need to study. I've been patient for several weeks." But the Spirit deflected every rationalizing move I made and pinned me to the mat with two realizations: I had harbored a judgmental spirit, and I had spoken inexcusable, harsh words.

So I went back later that evening and apologized, and in the weeks ahead, a strange thing began to happen. Every time I passed their room, instead of rehearsing their past offenses, I began to pray for them. The Spirit slowly began to melt the coldness I'd allowed to overtake my heart, and I grew to appreciate those two guys. Today I'm privileged to call them friends, and they both have fruitful ministries. But I couldn't manufacture that love on my own. Only the Spirit within me could make that happen.

3. *Self-Discipline to Endure Difficult Temptations.* The third Spirit-resource Paul mentions is self-discipline. The Greek word *sōphronismos* used here means to control of yourself in the face of passion. Whether the temptation is greed, lust, anger, or pride, the Spirit helps the believer overcome the vices that war against us.

How does the Spirit do this? The term "self-discipline" has within it the idea of "good judgment, wise thinking." The devil is a master deceiver, whispering lies to distort our thinking. He knows that when we believe a false reality, we behave in self-destructive ways. In this spiritual battle, the Spirit counters the lies by whispering truth, helping us to see life as it really is. When we perceive true reality, we can behave in self-disciplined ways.

Not only does the Spirit give us the *truth* that we need to rightly evaluate tempting moments, he also gives us the supernatural *discipline* we need to rightly act in those moments. Left to my own strength, I will too often choose wrong, even when I know it's wrong.

(Read Rom. 7:14–25.) In the face of temptation, I am profoundly unheroic. I am that skinny, fumbling, powerless eight-year-old Clark Kent all over again. That's why the Spirit's power is the only thing that will keep me going on when I feel like giving in.

No matter what foe you are facing—challenging circumstances, frustrating people, dark temptations—the Holy Spirit of God within you can transform you in heroic ways. When you emerge from God's telephone booth, you can stand tall with a big red *S* on your chest. It doesn't stand for Superman, but it does stand for "Spirit-filled." In the Holy Spirit, you have supernatural power. As you rely on him, you can finish strong.

> The Holy Spirit within you can transform you in heroic ways.

Discussion Questions

1. How comfortable are you talking about the Holy Spirit?
2. What do you think your spiritual gifts are?
3. Are you walking through anything right now that you need the power of the Holy Spirit to help you endure?
4. If the Holy Spirit gave you the ability to love the difficult people in your life, what would that look like practically?
5. What temptations do you need the Holy Spirit's power to endure?

TAKE ACTION Ask God to give you the spiritual resources you need to endure.

4

Meditate on the Gospel

2 Timothy 1:8–12

*"Men more frequently require to be
reminded than informed."*

— SAMUEL JOHNSON

Habituation.

My guess is you may not be familiar with this term. It's a phenomenon studied by psychologists. It happens when a new stimulus is introduced into your environment. At first, you're intensely aware of it. But over time, this awareness begins to fade, and you "habituate." For example, when you begin to wear a new wristwatch, you can feel it on your arm the first day or two. But within a few days, your nervous system "ignores" the weight of the watch, and you don't even know it's there. You have habituated.

Sometimes, out of long habit, we can ignore experiences that once sparked our amazement. On a trip to Yellowstone National Park, author Philip Yancey ate at a restaurant with large windows facing Old Faithful. When the famous geyser erupted, he noticed the patrons were drawn in wonder to the sight, but the servers continued their duties without even a glance toward the windows. It no longer captured their attention. They felt no awe. After a long familiarity, they had habituated.[1]

Spiritual Habituation

You have probably sung John Newton's hymn "Amazing Grace" many times, but here's my question: Are you still amazed by the gospel? Or have you habituated?

A few years ago, I accompanied our church's elementary kids to a local production of the *Passion Play*, a portrayal of Jesus' last week on earth. The group included several unchurched kids from a pretty rough neighborhood—street kids. I don't want to call them obnoxious, but let's just say that sitting politely for an hour in an auditorium waiting for the production to begin was not their spiritual gift. It was a Friday night. I was tired. I was riding herd on a third grader named David who kept harassing the other kids, being disruptive, and telling dirty jokes. I was ready for the evening to be over before the play even started.

Finally the lights went down, and to my surprise, within moments David was captivated, eyes wide with wonder. He had never heard the story of Jesus, so as the play unfolded, he kept asking me questions in the dark. Slowly I began to see the familiar story through David's fresh eyes.

When Jesus came down the aisle bearing his cross, within inches of where we sat, David was transfixed. The soldiers began pounding the nails, and David turned to me in genuine grief and asked, "Why are the soldiers doing that? Why are they killing him?"

I tried to explain simply, "Jesus hadn't done anything wrong. He let the soldiers kill him to take the punishment for our sins. Those other two men on the crosses were criminals. They died for the bad things they did. But Jesus died for the bad things *we* did."

David said, with tears in his eyes, "That's not fair!"

I gave the only reply I could. "You're right, David. It wasn't fair. But he did it because he loves us."

I offered him a tissue, and suddenly it hit me: it had been a long time since my heart was broken by the cross. When was the last time I wept at the foot of Calvary? I'd heard the story so many times that

I'd gotten used to it. Like the servers at the Old Faithful restaurant, long familiarity had drained my sense of wonder.

Sometimes the greatest danger we face is not spiritual rebellion. It's spiritual habituation.

Author Samuel Johnson once said that we don't need to be informed of new truths as much as reminded of old truths.[2] In 2 Timothy 1:8, Paul reminds Timothy of the gospel he has experienced. Paul knew that when we spiritually habituate, we no longer feel a sense of amazed thankfulness; we can take the gift of salvation for granted. Our motivation for persevering grows weak. We maximize our chances of finishing poorly when we minimize "so great a salvation" (Heb. 2:3).

> Sometimes the greatest danger is not spiritual rebellion. It's spiritual habituation.

But as Timothy meditates again on the gospel, Paul hopes the young man will be moved to gratitude. Psychological studies show that grateful people are more enthusiastic, more determined, and stronger.[3] Remembering our blessings can renew our spirits. When we are amazed again at God's love, we will be committed again to God's call.

As he challenges Timothy to suffer for the gospel, Paul reminds him of the gospel's content. What does this incredible gift from God include? In 2 Timothy 1:8–12, Paul lists three blessings for Timothy to consider: *grace for our past*, *hope for our future*, and *power for our present*.

Meditate on the Grace for Our Past

The first blessing is grace for our past. In 2 Timothy 1:9, Paul points to God's grace as the basis for our salvation. God has chosen us to be forgiven, washed clean, adopted as his children and the objects of his love. Is this because we are worthy—such wonderful people that of course he would want us? The answer is emphatically no. This word "grace" is often defined as, "*unmerited* favor."

No one is moral enough, nice enough, gifted enough to warrant God's attention or earn their salvation. We offer *absolutely* nothing. As Bishop William Temple once said, "The only thing of my very own which I contribute to redemption is the sin from which I need to be redeemed."[4]

This is the ugly fact: we are sinners, rebels (Rom. 3:23), and the punishment we deserve for our sin is death (Rom. 6:23).

But it is exactly at this point that God's grace enters. We all know the law of the universe is that you reap what you sow. It's what some call "karma": if you do bad stuff, then bad stuff eventually comes back to you. Because we have sinned, the natural result should be punishment. Grace, however, is the opposite of karma. In an illogical, unreasonable, surprising twist, God decides to interrupt the consequences of our actions. Instead of punishment, he offers forgiveness. Instead of wrath, he pours out love . . . all at the cost of his own Son (2 Tim. 1:9).

Don't miss this important fact: God made the decision to give us this astonishing grace "before the beginning of time" (1:9). Sometimes I cringe when I hear parents refer to an unexpected child as "our oops baby," as if they were an accident. But our arrival in God's family was not unplanned. We are not an accident or an afterthought. God wanted us so much that he planned Calvary before he prepared creation.

This is nothing short of incredible. Inexplicably, God decided from eternity past to trade the life of his perfect Son for a bunch of imperfect wretches. My third-grade friend David was right: this trade is not fair. But God made it with forethought, and he made it because he loves us. He wants us to be his.

Mary Ann Bird once experienced such grace. In her book *The Whisper Test* she writes:

> I grew up knowing I was different, and I hated it. I was born with a cleft palate, and when I started school, my classmates made it

clear to me how I looked to others: a little girl with a misshapen lip, crooked nose, lopsided teeth, and garbled speech.

When classmates asked, "What happened to your lip?" I'd tell them I'd fallen and cut it on a piece of glass. Somehow it seemed more acceptable to have suffered an accident than to have been born different. I was convinced that no one outside my family could love me.

There was, however, a teacher in the second grade whom we all adored—Mrs. Leonard by name. She was short, round, happy—a sparkling lady.

Annually we had a hearing test . . . Mrs. Leonard gave the test to everyone in the class, and finally it was my turn. I knew from past years that as we stood against the door and covered one ear, the teacher sitting at her desk would whisper something, and we would have to repeat it back—things like, "The sky is blue," or, "Do you have new shoes?" I waited there for those words that God must have put into her mouth, those seven words that changed my life. Mrs. Leonard said, in her whisper, "I wish you were my little girl."[5]

This is grace. Despite the fact that we are deeply marred by sin, God chooses us to be his children. He whispers, "I want you to be mine." Such a move is startling, unforeseen. Who could have guessed we were loved like *that*?

It turns out the gospel is not a to-do list to earn God's love. It is spelled D-O-N-E! The gospel is the joyous announcement that God already loves us. It is the good news that, in Jesus, he has already forgiven our sins. God's arms are thrown wide-open to receive us, and all we have to do is walk into his embrace.

> The gospel is the joyous announcement that God already loves us.

I'm betting that as Timothy read these words from Paul, he whispered one word as he shook his head: *Amazing.*

Meditate on the Hope for Our Future

The second blessing Paul lists in 2 Timothy 1:8–12 is hope for our future. Since Genesis 3, the future of humankind has been summed up in a single word: death. It is the destiny of us all. Statistics show that one out of every one human being dies. No one escapes. Death is, quite simply, our greatest enemy. The scoreboard of history reads Death: 100 billion / Humanity: 0.

But then came Jesus. In 2 Timothy 1:10, Paul pictures Christ in hand-to-hand combat with death. On Good Friday, the battle was joined, and at first it looked like death had triumphed again. At the end of the day, Christ was dead—no pulse, lifeless, cold. He lay dead in the tomb Friday night. He lay there dead Saturday morning. He lay there dead Saturday night.

But then came Sunday morning. As the first rays of dawn broke over the horizon, a voice came rumbling in on the wind—a whisper from God piercing the walls of that garden tomb: "Arise, my Son."

As those words echoed deep inside that cave, something happened. A heart that was still as the grave suddenly began to beat again. Blood, thick and cold, rushed warmly through veins. A chest heaved upward, taking in a great breath. Stiff fingers moved, eyes opened, arms raised, legs swung off the table—he was standing again. Jesus Christ had risen!

In all previous resurrections in the Bible—the Shunammite's boy, the widow of Nain's son, Lazarus—they came back to life only to someday die again. But the resurrection of Jesus Christ was not a momentary victory. In 2 Timothy 1:10, Paul says Christ "destroyed death." He had broken its power, and death could never again claim him. The scoreboard now read, Death: 100 billion / Humanity: 1.

That score will someday change. The Bible is clear that Christ's resurrection was a preview of coming attractions (1 Cor. 15:20–23). If we belong to him, someday we too will be raised from the dead to "life and immortality" (1:10). We will live never to die again.

And what a life it will be! The word "immortality" here actually means "incorruptibility." Right now we live in a world corrupted by sin and death and time. Let's just think of the effects of time. With the passing days, cars rust, fruit rots, and our bodies break down. The second law of thermodynamics—the universe is running down—gets us all. Time is not our friend.

My grandpa was a farmer and could work from sunup to sundown—a strong and strapping man in his day. But as the years went by, he moved more slowly. His hearing and eyesight dimmed; his back was weak. His body suffered the effects of a corrupted world.

But what if we lived in an incorruptible world? If there is time in eternity, what if it somehow works backward? What if every day is fresher and brighter than the one before? The second law of thermodynamics is suddenly reversed, and everything gets better with time. Fruit gets sweeter, clothes get newer, floors get cleaner. Every morning in the new heavens and new earth, my grandpa will wake up to work in the fields he loved, and he will feel stronger and healthier and younger than the day before. We will be raised to experience "immortality"—the incredible hope of a world uncorrupted by sin and death and even time itself (1 Cor. 15:42).

For the Christian, death is no longer the end of the road, but a bend in the road. It is no longer the period at the end of the sentence of life, but a comma—transitioning us from this life to the next. Jesus kicked the end out of the tomb and turned it into a tunnel to eternal life!

This hope gives us the strength to persevere. In the Muslim-majority nation of Indonesia, persecuted believers encourage one another with a saying: "We have suffering for breakfast, perseverance for lunch, and victory in Jesus for dinner." The apostle Peter said that we have "a living hope through the resurrection of Jesus Christ from the dead, and . . . . In this you greatly rejoice, though now for a little while you may have had to suffer grief in all kinds of trials" (1 Pet. 1:3–6). No matter the difficulties we face, we know how our story will end. If we finish, we win.

I'm betting that as Timothy meditated on this deep hope, he once again shook his head and whispered: *Amazing.*

Meditate on the Power for Our Present

Paul mentions one final blessing in the gift of salvation: power for the present. In 2 Timothy 1:8, Paul tells Timothy that the power to endure his present suffering will come from God. On the heels of 1:7, Paul is likely referring to the power of the Holy Spirit, which we discussed in the last chapter. The indwelling Holy Spirit is part of God's gift of salvation, and it is the Spirit who gives believers the strength to live each day for God.

You'll notice that Paul concludes the passage with his own example of empowered endurance. He describes his ministry with three words, calling himself:

- A *herald:* someone who makes announcements on behalf of the king. It's translated elsewhere as "preacher" (2 Pet. 2:5). Paul's ministry included *proclaiming* the gospel.
- An *apostle:* someone chosen directly by Christ to speak with Christ's authority. Thus the Twelve, plus Paul, were the official keepers of sound doctrine. Paul's ministry included *guarding* the gospel.
- A *teacher:* someone who gives instruction on Christian doctrine and its ethical implications. The early church didn't have the New Testament yet, with its descriptions of a Christian life. So Paul's ministry included *explaining* the gospel.

Paul had a lot to do! Of course, he had to do all this heralding and "apostling" and teaching in the midst of hardships like imprisonment, shipwrecks, and stonings. How did he endure?

The simple answer: by trusting God to get him through. In verse twelve, Paul says he is "convinced" that God is powerful enough to guard "what I have entrusted to him"—namely, his own life. In other words, *I put my life in God's hands, and God's hands are strong enough to take care of me.* Paul had the track record to prove it:

- When he was shipwrecked, God's power rescued him.
- When he was stoned, God's power raised him back up.

- When he was imprisoned, God's power sustained him.
- When he was targeted by assassins, God's power protected him.
- When he was physically weak, God's power carried him.[6]

Paul wants Timothy to know: what God has done for me, he will do for you. He is saying, *Don't forget, Timothy. Remember again the Mighty Presence who makes himself available to you. The same Holy Spirit who strengthens me will strengthen you. The same Father who has given me power to endure will also empower you.*

In the 1992 Summer Olympics in Barcelona, Derek Redmond of Great Britain was a favorite for a medal in the 400-meter race. The runners lined up, the gun sounded, and Derek quickly seized the lead. But with 175 meters to go, Derek suddenly pulled up and fell to the track, clutching his right leg. He had pulled his hamstring. The other runners finished, and tears began to stream down his face. It appeared his Olympic dream was over.

Up in the stands, Derek's father, Jim, watched in disbelief. Immediately he began racing down from the top row to the track, bumping some people and sidestepping others in his hurry. Later he told the press, "I wasn't going to be stopped by anyone."

Down on the track, Derek Redmond grimaced in pain, but he refused the medical crew with the stretcher. Instead, in a moment that will live forever in my mind, Derek lifted himself to his feet and began to hobble down the track, hopping on one leg. He was not limping to the side of the track to drop out. No, he was going to finish the race on one leg. He would cross that finish line. The crowd stood to their feet and began to cheer, then roar.

Derek hobbled on, each step slower than the last, his face twisted in pain. Then unexpectedly, another figure ran onto the track behind him. Jim Redmond had leapt over the railing, evading security, and was now running alongside Derek. The father put his arm around the son, and the son collapsed momentarily, sobbing into the father's shoulder. Together, arm in arm—with 65,000 people clapping, cheering, and crying—father and son finished the race.

The Father gives us the strength to finish the race.

In the press and fury of our lives, we sometimes forget. We habituate.

But Paul tells Timothy and tells us: don't forget. Meditate again on the incredible gift of salvation—grace for our past, hope for our future, and power for our present. We can endure the hardships and cross the finish line—not in our own power, but in his.

I'm betting that as Timothy remembered the power now at work within him, he shook his head and again whispered: *Amazing.*

Discussion Questions

1. What used to excite or amaze you about God that you've now grown too familiar with?
2. Go through the Ten Commandments (Exod. 20:3–17) and count how many you've never broken. What was your score? How does this exercise make you feel?
3. How has death touched your life? How does the hope of resurrection change your thinking about death?
4. Think about a time when you experienced God's power in your life. How did knowing he was with you fuel you?

TAKE ACTION Thank God for his power in your life.

5

Guard the Truth

2 Timothy 1:13–2:2

"The torch of heavenly light must be transmitted unquenched from one generation to another."

— E. K. SIMPSON

One of a soldier's highest honors is standing guard at the Tomb of the Unknown Soldier. At Arlington National Cemetery outside of Washington, D.C., each sentinel takes his task seriously, honoring those who gave their lives to protect America's freedom. They call their continuous march in front of the tomb "walking the mat."

The tomb has been guarded twenty-four hours a day, seven days a week since July 1937. Tomb guards walk the mat in good weather and bad, without fail, without complaint, and without change of expression.

On the night of September 18, 2003, Hurricane Isabel pounded the capital, but the guard continued to walk the mat. For the first time ever, the sentinels were given permission to seek safety inside, in the trophy room.

None left.

Sergeant First Class Frederick Geary heard a sharp cracking sound, but he did not flinch as an old tree collapsed just two dozen yards from where he marched. Though the hurricane winds felled at least twenty-four trees, Sgt. Geary led the charge to keep the sentinels on the black mat. "We made the decision to stand where we were," he said. Looking at the Tomb of the Unknown Soldier, he choked up, "They did their job. We have a job to do here. I was just doing what I believed to be right."[1] Another sentinel, Sergeant Christopher Holmes, insisted that this is "the greatest honor."[2]

In 2 Timothy 1:13–2:2, Paul essentially tells his disciple, *Timothy, you have been entrusted with the highest honor—guarding the gospel. You stand as a sentinel outside an empty tomb—Jesus Christ's victory over sin and the grave. Nothing is more valuable than this gospel. Guard it with your life! Even when storms cause others to abandon their post, stand firm.*

Paul has guarded the gospel given to him, and now he challenges Timothy to hold the gospel tight. Timothy must not relax his grip, and he must not let it drop. Finishing well means guarding God's truth, and in these verses, Paul describes how we do this.

Specifically, Paul describes three ways the gospel should be guarded: *doctrinal defense* to protect the content of the gospel, *personal sacrifice* to protect the value of the gospel, and *relational investment* to protect the continuation of the gospel.

Guard the Gospel Through Doctrinal Defense

Paul calls Timothy to protect the content of the gospel through doctrinal defense. In 1:13–14, Paul uses two vivid expressions to describe the gospel. First, he says it's a "pattern" of sound teaching. The Greek word for pattern—*hypotypōsis*—has in it the idea of "an outline sketch such as an architect might make . . . of a building."[3] Timothy is not to allow anyone to "remodel" or "add on" to the gospel. He must ensure that the original blueprint is followed.

The second expression for the gospel is "the good deposit" (*parathēkē*). In ancient Greece, a man could give an inheritance to a friend that would be kept for his children, or he might deposit his valuables in a temple (the banks of the ancient world) for safe keeping. In each case, the deposit was called a *parathēkē*. William Barclay writes, "In the ancient world, there was no more sacred duty than the safe-guarding of such a deposit and the returning of it when in due time it was claimed."[4]

Timothy, then, was to guard the gospel as a sacred treasure. The word "guard" is used elsewhere for guarding a palace against marauders and possessions against thieves (Luke 11:21; Acts 22:20). He must defend the gospel against the heretics in Ephesus who attempted to spoil the gospel treasure that God entrusted to his people.

There is still a need today to defend the "pattern of sound teaching." Many—from both inside and outside the church—seek to corrupt the gospel. In one of the churches I served, a young couple became enamored with a popular televangelist. They watched his program and even sent money to his organization.

Unfortunately, this man was a false teacher. He taught that when people become Christians, they can make things happen simply by speaking the words with enough faith. The (incorrect) idea is that just as God spoke things into existence, we can too. This is sometimes called "name it and claim it" theology.

Sadly, the young couple began to apply his teaching to their new business. I sat down with them to express my concerns, but my warning fell on deaf ears. When their business faltered, their faith did as well. Thankfully, they eventually realized their error and returned to the gospel.

The stakes are high here. We live in a world where the gospel is threatened by those who change its teachings on sexual ethics, Jesus' identity, the authority of Scripture, the sovereignty of God, salvation requirements, and much more. By the way, heresy can take two forms: requiring less *or* more than the gospel does. Both permissiveness and legalism "remodel" the original apostolic blueprint, and we must confront such false teaching. It's always more enjoyable to share encouraging truth than to confront potential errors. But when the eternities of others are at stake, we have to learn to confront.

In guarding the gospel, Timothy is protecting his flock.

Guard the Gospel Through Personal Sacrifice

Guarding the gospel certainly requires doctrinal defense. But it also demands personal sacrifice. Such sacrifice protects the value of the gospel: it shows that the gospel is so valuable it is worth suffering for. Standing up for the gospel can come with a high cost—ridicule, rejection, even physical persecution—and sometimes we can be reluctant to pay the price.

I once spent a year working with Bob Russell, then senior minister of Southeast Christian Church in Louisville, Kentucky. Bob took bold stands on biblical truth, but he shared with me how one time he had taken the easy way out. As the leader of a megachurch, Bob was often asked to pray at community events. Once, at a civic function, the organizer found him a few minutes before the invocation. "Remember that we have people from many different backgrounds here," she said.

Bob understood what she was asking: give a generic prayer to avoid offending those of other faiths. He began with "Dear Father"— safe ground because many religions use those terms. The problem, Bob knew, would be the ending. Because Jesus said, "My Father will give you whatever you ask in my name," Christians have traditionally closed their prayers with "in Jesus' name" (John 16:23).

Bob ended, "I pray these things in the name of the Lion of the Tribe of Judah. Amen." He sat down feeling smug—he had prayed in Jesus' name and almost nobody knew it! Reflecting back, Bob said, "Some might call that creativity, but I call that cowardice. I wimped out. After that, I decided I would always pray 'in Jesus' name.' I've noticed two results: I feel better about my witness, and I get fewer invitations to pray!" The fact is that, at best, identifying with Jesus can be unpopular. At worst, it can be downright dangerous. That was certainly true for persecuted Christians in the first century. When Paul was arrested, many turned their backs on him, and perhaps even on Christianity. At one point, he says, "Everyone in the province of Asia has deserted me" (2 Tim. 1:15). The gospel is free, but it is not cheap.

> **The gospel is free, but it is not cheap.**

But thank the Lord, Paul at least had Onesiphorus, a man from Ephesus. These men had grown close, and Onesiphorus loved Paul. He was a constant help to him, often opening his home to the apostle to offer much-needed refreshment.

Even when Paul was in prison, Onesiphorus did not turn his back on his friend. He was a living example of the exhortation that Paul gave to Timothy: "Do not be ashamed of the testimony about our Lord or of me his prisoner" (1:8). Onesiphorus traveled the 1,200 miles from Ephesus to Rome, and when he arrived in the great city, he tramped through the streets and alleys, government buildings and ghettoes, searching for Paul until he found him.

Understand: there was great risk in associating with an enemy of the Empire. As one commentator writes, "It was dangerous to keep asking where a certain criminal could be found; it was dangerous to visit him; it was still more dangerous to keep on visiting him; but that is what Onesiphorus did."[5] Why would Onesiphorus make such a personal sacrifice? Because of the bond he shared with Paul *in the gospel.* He was committed to Paul because he was committed to Jesus. Sometimes the way we guard the gospel is simply by not letting go of it when the gospel is inconvenient or even risky.

Throughout our world, many are making personal sacrifices because they are unwilling to let the gospel be compromised:

- A Christian psychologist in Michigan is fired after she declines to counsel a gay couple about their relationship.
- A university professor in Iowa loses his job because of his stand on the biblical view of creation.
- A Chinese pastor is imprisoned for preaching the truth about Jesus.
- A Christian college student in Nigeria refuses to renounce her faith in Christ and is stoned and burned alive.

This is what you'd call "personal sacrifice" for identifying with Jesus. But the good news is that as God's people, we don't have to suffer in our own strength. In both 1:14 and 2:1, Paul reminds Timothy that the Spirit of Christ within him will give him the strength he needs.

At some point, you may be called on to sacrifice for the sake of the gospel. Are you willing to pay the price? I once heard a pastor share about visiting the Lincoln Memorial. He stopped at a store across the street to check out the souvenirs and picked up a little bronze replica of the World War II Memorial to the Marines who fought at Iwo Jima. The disinterested man behind the counter suddenly perked up, sensing a potential sale. "Cheap!" he said with a smile. "Only ten dollars!"

My friend nodded, put the bronze replica back, and walked on, thinking to himself, *No, not cheap. Not cheap at all.* In thirty-six days of fighting, the Marines sustained more than 25,000 casualties on Iwo Jima—including 7,000 fatalities. There was nothing cheap about it. As Americans, these men received their freedom at no cost, but to defend that freedom, they paid a great price.

Likewise, as Christians we receive the gospel at no cost, but to defend that gospel, we may have to pay a great price. The gospel is free, but it is not cheap.

Guard the Gospel Through Relational Investment

If doctrinal defense protects the gospel's content and personal sacrifice protects the gospel's value, then relational investment protects the gospel's continuation. In 2 Timothy 2:2, Paul describes this third way Timothy is to guard the gospel—investing in the next generation of gospel teachers. He challenges Timothy to mentor future leaders: "And the things you have heard me say in the presence of many witnesses entrust to reliable people who will also be qualified to teach others."

E. K. Simpson wrote, "The torch of heavenly light must be transmitted unquenched from one generation to another."[6] Notice the stages in the faithful transmission of the gospel from one generation to the next:

- The transmission from Christ to Paul. In Galatians 1:10–11, Paul writes, "The gospel I preached . . . I received . . . by revelation from Jesus Christ."
- The transmission from Paul to Timothy. Timothy heard Paul teach the gospel "in the presence of many witnesses."
- The transmission from Timothy to "reliable people." Paul said they must be men who could be counted on to guard the gospel.
- The transmission from "reliable people" to "others."

Of course, these "others" will also pass the gospel on to the next generation and so on, all the way to the present time. Think about this heritage. The one who stands up in your church next Sunday to teach, according to Barclay, "is a link in the living chain which stretches unbroken from this present moment back to Jesus Christ."[7]

This living chain is essential if we are to guard the truth of God's Word from one generation to the next. We must be highly intentional about praying for, supporting, and training up the next wave of gospel leaders and teachers because it is so easy for "truth decay" to happen in the generational exchange. As I once heard a preacher say, "What one generation defends, the next assumes, and the next neglects." So how can this leadership mentoring take place? I'll offer four practical suggestions.

1. *Recognize that leadership training is a priority (whether you're the trainer or the trainee).* There is no success without a successor. No matter how impressive your accomplishments, you have only "built to last" if you have prepared those who will continue your spiritual legacy when you are gone. As my high school track coach told my 4x800 meter relay team, "Races are won or lost at the passing of the baton."

> Races are won or lost at the passing of the baton.

That's why we must spend significant time entrusting the work of the gospel to, as Paul said, "reliable people." Journalist Walter Lippmann once wrote, "The final test of a leader is that he leaves behind in other men the conviction and will to carry on."[8] Make this a priority.

2. *Look for potential future leaders.* They may be eloquent or slow of speech, five-talent or one-talent people, A+ or C- students. God has given the gifts of leadership and teaching to all kinds of people. (See 1 Cor. 1:26–27.)

3. *Build a relationship.* Paul invested deeply in his relationship with Timothy—just as Jesus did with his disciples. When you find a potential disciple, get to know them, spend time with them, and genuinely care about them. Dr. Lynn Gardner was the academic dean at Ozark Christian College when I began teaching there. I was just twenty-six years old—barely shaving! I wasn't sure how I would be received by the other faculty, including some who had been there longer than I'd been alive. Thankfully, they welcomed me with open arms, especially Dr. Gardner. He once said to me, "The way I figure it, we're supposed to be more like the old horse than the old dog. The old dog is afraid the young dog will get his bone, but the old horse is glad for the young horse because he can help carry the load."

Dr. Gardner sure acted like he was glad I was there. He made a point to talk to me in the hallway or in the library. He'd go out of his way to pass on little pieces of wit and wisdom, recommend a good book, or tell me a story of his early teaching days. After I preached in chapel, Dr. Gardner told me he appreciated my sermon. When I was staying too many hours on campus that first year of teaching, he encouraged me to go home and be with my family.

I knew he cared, so I listened when he spoke. A mentor will build a relationship.

4. *Teach them what you know.* If you're a Sunday school teacher or small group leader, show apprentices how to prepare a lesson or lead a discussion. If you're a preacher, teach them how to write a sermon. If you're an elder, take them with you on a hospital call. Get them involved with you and look for opportunities to share what you've learned through the years about Scripture and life. Talk to

them about the essentials of the faith and study the Bible together. Urge them to remain true to the gospel.

The British evangelist Leonard Ravenhill tells of a tourist in a European village who asked a local, "Were any great men born in this village?" The local replied, "Nope. Only babies."[9] The fact is, leaders are made, not born. Leaders don't suddenly appear, fully developed. They will have to be taught. As you teach them, you are guarding the gospel, preserving and proclaiming it in the next generation.

An Unlikely Looking Sentinel

For thirty-five years, Henrietta Mears taught the college Sunday school class at the large First Presbyterian Church in Hollywood, California. Standing at five feet and four inches, thickset with "coke-bottle" glasses and a deep love for Christ, this passionate woman sent out more than four hundred young men and women into Christian service, including eventual US Senate Chaplain Richard Halverson, Young Life founder Jim Rayburn, and Cru founder Bill Bright.

At one point, a young, largely unknown evangelist named Billy Graham sought out Miss Mears. The winds of liberal theology were howling in the late 1940s, and one of Billy's closest evangelist friends had abandoned his belief in the infallibility of Scripture. Billy was questioning his own beliefs.

Though Henrietta looked nothing like one of the sentinels at the Tomb of the Unknown Soldier, she held her ground just as staunchly as the guards during Hurricane Isabel. She talked to Billy about reasons for believing in the Bible's infallibility. She refused to compromise or conform to current theological thought. Her gentle but strong convictions made a deep impression on young Graham as he stood at a faith crossroads, and he decided that he too would hold to orthodox Christianity. It was immediately after his decision that Billy Graham's Los Angeles crusade catapulted him to worldwide recognition and ministry. Praise God for a five-foot-four-inch defender of the faith named Henrietta!

The truth is too important, the stakes are too high, the threat is too real for us to abandon our post. Stand strong when the storms of doubt and error rage. You have been entrusted with a high and sacred honor.

Guard the gospel.

Discussion Questions

1. What would you say are the essential elements of the gospel?
2. Where is our culture seeking to undermine the clear teaching of Scripture?
3. Have you ever experienced false teaching?
4. In what ways might you have to personally sacrifice for the sake of the gospel?
5. What could you personally do to help raise up the next generation of disciples?

TAKE ACTION Ask God for the courage to stand firm for the gospel's truth.

6

Expect Tough Times

2 Timothy 2:3–13

"Stick-to-it-iveness is an important Christian virtue. As one preacher used to say, 'There are three abilities: know-ability, do-ability and stick-ability. And the greatest of these is stick.'"

— SETH WILSON

When the going gets tough, the tough get going." More often, however, we simply want the "tough going" to go away. A few years ago, hikers in the Bridger-Teton National Forest left the following actual comments in a suggestion box:

- Trail needs to be reconstructed. Please avoid building trails that go uphill.
- Too many bugs and leaches and spiders and spider webs. Please spray the wilderness to rid the area of these pests.
- Chairlifts need to be installed so we can get to wonderful views without having to hike to them.
- Please pave the trails. Too many rocks in the mountains.
- A small deer came into my camp and stole my jar of pickles. Is there a way I can get reimbursed?

Sometimes we are, as one book title suggests, "a nation of wimps."[1] Let's face it—the natural human response to suffering is to avoid it. In Mark 4:16–17, Jesus predicted that when the going got tough for some new Christians, they would want to quit: "When trouble or persecution comes because of the word, they quickly fall away."

In 2 Timothy 2:3–13, Paul wants Timothy to know two things: the Christian life is *really hard*—and *really worth it*.

Three Pictures of Endurance

Paul begins the passage with three metaphors that Timothy is to "reflect on" (2:7). Bible teacher Warren Wiersbe said the human mind is not a debating hall; it's a picture gallery.[2] We most often think in pictures, images, and metaphors—and our mental metaphors matter because those images create expectations that influence our behavior. If you think being a Christian is more like being a Boy Scout than being a soldier, then when bullets start flying, you might abandon your post and go AWOL.

In 2:3–6, Paul tells Timothy who he is, using three "role metaphors." The apostle hangs three images in Timothy's mental picture gallery, and each one carries with it some expectation of difficulty.

1. *Soldier.* In 2:3, Paul compares Timothy to a soldier. Paul knew something about Roman soldiers, having spent a considerable portion of his life guarded by them! He knew that a Roman solder was a picture of complete dedication. There were no "weekend warriors"—they were required to sign on for a twenty-year hitch. To avoid civilian distractions, they were forbidden to marry (2:4). Only half of all Roman soldiers survived to retirement, so every soldier knew to expect hardship. This was no nine-to-five job. A Roman soldier ate, drank, breathed, slept, lived, and died doing his duty as a soldier.

In fact, the word "endure" in 2:3 (NLT) was a military word used to describe a soldier holding position. The Greek term *hupomonē*—literally "remain under"—meant stay at your post, stand your ground, stick to your guns—like the soldier at Pompeii. When the eruption of Mt. Vesuvius destroyed the Italian city of Pompeii in AD 79, many people were immediately buried in the volcanic ash, preserved in their final frozen moment of terror. Amazingly, ruins of a Roman sentinel were found at the city gate, his hands still grasping his weapon. He had been placed there by his captain, and though the earth shook beneath him, as the fiery rain of ashes overwhelmed him, he stood at his post. He was found there, standing a thousand years later—faithful even in death. That's *hupomonē*.

A soldier doesn't know the word "quit." Some believers today are like the kamikaze pilot who flew fifty missions. (Think about that.) They want to be involved, but not committed. As I heard one preacher say, "Too many Christians want the medals, but they don't want the scars."

I want to be a soldier like Art Chen. Art Chen was a Chinese fighter pilot in the 1930s when China was at war with Japan. In one battle, he took on three Japanese fighter planes. He shot one down, then ran out of ammunition, so he deliberately rammed into a second plane, disabling it, and then parachuted out of his own plane. He landed close to the wreckage of his plane and managed to salvage one of the heavy machine guns from it.

He hoisted the heavy gun up on his shoulder and carried it eight miles back to his air base. When he arrived, Art found his commanding officer, dropped the big gun in front of him, and said, "Sir, can I have another airplane for my machine gun?"

That's a soldier who doesn't know the word "quit." Paul says, "Timothy, that's who you are. When you look in the mirror, that's a soldier looking back. Soldiers expect hardship, and soldiers don't quit."

2. Athlete. In 2:5, Paul compares Timothy to an athlete. Paul was apparently a sports fan and often used athletic imagery to describe the Christian life—including running (Gal. 2:2), boxing (1 Cor. 9:26), wrestling (Eph. 6:12), gladiatorial contests (1 Cor. 4:9), and chariot races (Phil. 3:13–14). Here, Paul says that an athlete wins by "competing according to the rules" (2:5). That phrase refers to the oath every Olympic athlete had to take, pledging to enter ten months of strict training before the Games. Before these athletes could win the crown, they had to push themselves through the suffering. An athlete understood that hardship was part of the package.

This is still true today. Athletes push themselves with the motto, "No pain, no gain." (My personal motto is, "No pain, no pain.") Athletes expect difficulty. When a running back gets tackled, he doesn't get up whining to the defense, "What did you do that for? Nobody told me I was going to get hit." If you're a football player, you know that if you carry the ball, you're going to get tackled.

Paul's point is that Christians ought to expect difficulty. First Peter 4:12 tells us, "Do not be surprised at the fiery ordeal that has come on you to test you, as though something strange were happening to you." And 2 Timothy 3:12 promises that "everyone who wants to live a godly life in Christ Jesus will be persecuted." If you thought becoming a Christian would solve all your problems, think again. Hardship is part of the package. But as spiritual athletes, we push through it. We run all the way across the finish line.

I'm a sucker for courageous sports stories—tales of athletes who heroically persevere through pain:

- After his jaw was broken, Muhammad Ali fought ten more rounds, finishing a bout with Ken Norton.
- In the 1997 NBA Finals game five, Michael Jordan's severe flu made him look like death warmed over, but he wound up scoring thirty-eight points, including the game-winning basket.
- In high school, Heisman Trophy winner Tim Tebow once played the entire second half of a football game on a broken leg, even running in a twenty-nine-yard touchdown!

Paul is saying to Timothy and to you, *This is who you are. When you look in the mirror, that's an athlete looking back. Athletes expect hardship, and athletes don't quit.*

3. *Farmer.* Paul also compares Timothy to a farmer (2:6). I have worked on a farm, and it can be hard physical labor, long hours, heavy loads. But think: Paul is writing before the days of air-conditioned tractor cabs and hydraulic forklifts. A farmer in the ancient world lived an even more difficult life. Paul calls farmers "hardworking," and that word *kopiaō* paints pictures of sweat and struggle, bent back

and straining muscles, exertion and exhaustion. As commentator John Stott points out, "Unlike the soldier and the athlete, the farmer's life is totally devoid of excitement, remote from all glamour of peril and of applause."[3]

But a farmer, both then and now, knew that if they didn't work, their family didn't eat. So, hard as it was, a farmer didn't quit. He kept working. While *kopiaō* usually referred to manual labor, Paul uses the word in other places to describe the spiritual work of a Christian. In Romans 16:6, he mentions "Mary, who *worked very hard* for you." In 1 Timothy 5:17, he comments on elders "whose *work* is preaching and teaching." In 2 Corinthians 6:5, Paul lists his leadership credentials as "beatings, imprisonments and riots . . . *hard work*, sleepless nights and hunger."

This level of persistent work is part of being a Christian and a Christian leader. Paul is saying, *Timothy, this is who you are. When you look in the mirror, that's a farmer looking back. Farmers expect hardship, and farmers don't quit.*

Three Purposes of Endurance

With each of these three metaphors, Paul hints at a reward for endurance. A soldier gets a medal after pleasing his commanding officer (2:4). An athlete wins a crown after competing according to the rules (2:5). A farmer reaps a harvest after working hard in the fields (2:6).

In other words, Paul is saying that the Christian life is *really hard*—and *really worth it*. He wants to remind us that we do not labor in vain. Joe Namath, the famous New York Jets quarterback, once famously said, "When you win, nothing hurts." We endure hardship more readily when we recognize some worthwhile purpose behind it. The Jewish psychiatrist and Holocaust survivor Viktor Frankl wrote, "He who has a *why* to live can bear with almost any *how*."[4]

So what exactly is the *why* of the Christian life? What is the reward for enduring difficult times? What purposes does it accomplish? In 2:8–13, Paul mentions three reasons for persevering:

1. *You become more like Christ.* Maybe you've heard the story of the two little boys at the breakfast table. Kevin was eight, Ryan was five, and they were fighting over who would get the first pancake. Seeing a teachable moment, their mother sat down and said, "You know, if Jesus were sitting here, he would say, 'Let my brother have the first pancake.'" So Kevin turned to his little brother and said, "Okay, Ryan . . . you be Jesus!"

As Christians, we say we want to be like Jesus, but are we willing to endure hardship to see it happen? In 2:8, Paul writes, "Remember Jesus Christ, raised from the dead, descended from David." Notice the order of those last two phrases. Before Paul references the kingship of Christ ("descended from David"), he mentions the cross of Christ ("raised from the dead"). Before the crown of gold came the crown of thorns. Before Christ's sovereignty came his suffering. Paul is reminding Timothy that Jesus himself had to endure hard times. So when we endure hardships, we are becoming like Jesus.

> When we endure hardships, we are becoming like Jesus.

The ancient Christian writer Tertullian said, "The man who is afraid to suffer cannot belong to him who suffered."[5] Jesus himself said in John 15:20, "The servant is not greater than his lord. If they have persecuted me, they will also persecute you." If we choose to walk in the footsteps of Jesus, we will wind up walking up a hill to a cross. As Daniel Berrigan famously said, "If you want to follow Jesus, you'd better look good on wood."

Not only does living a life of sacrifice connect us to the experience of Christ, it also conforms us to the character of Christ. The simple act of persevering can grow us toward spiritual maturity. James 1:4 says, "Let perseverance finish its work so that you may be mature and complete, not lacking anything."

In one survey, hundreds of people were asked to identify the factors that were most formative in their spiritual growth. The top response overwhelmingly involved times of suffering and pain.[6] A few weeks ago, I spoke with a man whose son died of a terrible disease at age fifteen. He said, "If I had it to do over, I would not have wanted this tragedy to happen, but neither would I want to be the man I was before it happened."

The act of holding onto Jesus through painful times draws us closer to him, so don't quit.

2. You bring people to Christ. A second purpose for endurance is that God may use your steadfastness to bring people to himself. In 2:9–10, Paul says he is "suffering even to the point of being chained like a criminal. But . . . I endure everything for the sake of the elect, that they too may obtain the salvation that is in Christ Jesus, with eternal glory." Paul is willing to endure trials if it means he can help introduce people to Jesus.

Sometimes the greatest witness to a lost world is not persuasive speechmaking, ironclad evidence, or dramatic testimony. It's simply a life lived faithfully, through good times and bad, over the long haul.

One of my students preaches in Irwin, Missouri, population thirty-five. The Irwin church is just a handful of loyal saints, including Thelma. Thelma is almost ninety, hard of hearing, and can't get out when it's colder than forty-five degrees. But Thelma hasn't retired from service.

When Thelma heard that her neighbor Denise was diagnosed with lupus, she baked a plate of cookies and slowly walked down the street to Denise's house. Because of Thelma's simple act of compassion, Denise is now a part of the Irwin church—and so are Denise's family members: Daniel, A. J., Amanda, Isaac, Jacob, and Debbie. Thelma's loving witness almost doubled the church's membership!

Thelma can't do much now at ninety years old, but one thing she won't do is quit. Sometimes it's not the wattage of our light that makes the difference. It's the fact that it keeps shining no matter what happens. You don't have to be a halogen floodlight. God can work through twenty-five-watt people who refuse to burn out.

Paul is saying, we "endure everything" to win some. Timothy must keep loving, keep serving, keep working, keep praying, keep speaking, keep persevering, keep shining because somewhere along the line, God might use something he does to usher someone into the kingdom.

You never know: he might use something *you* do, so don't quit.

3. *You save your seat with Christ.* In verses 11–13, Paul quotes what he calls "a trustworthy saying." This is one of five "trustworthy sayings" scattered throughout what are called the Pastoral Epistles (1 Tim. 1:15; 3:1; 4:9; and Titus 3:8). These sayings were apparently creeds or hymns often used in the early church—material already familiar to the apostle's readers.

This ancient hymn contains four stanzas, each starting with the word "if," and each stanza focuses on God's response to a different situation.

- The first stanza is God's response to a believer's *conversion.* "If we died with him" refers to our death with Christ in the waters of baptism (see Rom. 6:4). When we make the initial choice to follow Christ, God gives us the hope of new life, both in this world and in the world to come.
- The second stanza is God's response to a believer's *endurance.* If, after that initial decision, we remain true to Christ, God will welcome us into heaven someday and allow us to reign alongside Christ forever. Wow! I'll return to this theme in a moment.
- The third stanza is God's response to a believer's *disavowal.* When a believer finally and fully turns their back on God, God has no choice but to turn his back finally as well. This is the same kind of warning Jesus gave in Matthew 10:33: "Whoever disowns me before others, I will disown before my Father in heaven."
- The fourth stanza is God's response to a believer's *failure.* "Faithless" here does not refer to a complete lack of faith, but a wavering faith (see Mark 9:24). Stanza three deals with a person's permanent rejection of God, but this fourth stanza deals with a believer's temporary lapse into disobedience. If stanza three describes Judas's once-for-all betrayal, stanza four

describes Peter's momentary denial. Here, God promises to be faithful to such a person, despite their failings. As 1 John 1:9 says, "If we confess our sins, he is faithful and just and will forgive us our sins and purify us from all unrighteousness." If a prodigal son returns, God welcomes him back with open arms.

The big idea of the hymn is this: God sticks by those who stick by him. What exactly does God do for those who endure? He saves them a seat with him in heaven someday. By the way, that seat is a throne! The promise of 2 Timothy 2:12 is that we will reign with Christ forever.[7] Though now on this earth we are sometimes outcasts, in heaven we shall be royalty.

> **God sticks by those who stick by him.**

When my daughter Lydia was five, she wanted desperately to be royalty. Lydia's kindergarten teacher made a photo album of her students, and each child's page included their answers to a list of questions. One question was, "What do you want to be when you grow up?" The other children's answers were predictable: doctor, teacher, nurse, truck driver. Lydia, however, was the only one who answered, "queen."

She loved dressing up in gowns and crowns, swishing around the house, receiving the applause of her adoring subjects. Lydia couldn't watch enough of those Disney movies like *Sleeping Beauty* and *Cinderella* and *Beauty and the Beast*—where the princess swirls around the ballroom, dances with the prince, marries him, and lives happily ever after. She really wanted to be royalty.

She's older now, but I don't ever want her to lose that.

I know that as Lydia grows up, she will go through hard times. She will face trials and tribulations, and at some point, she will feel like giving up.

But I want her to know that someday, if she holds on, she will inherit a kingdom wealthier than any earthly kingdom.

She will live in a palace more beautiful than Disney could ever draw.

At the wedding banquet of the Lamb, she will not just dance with the prince. If she endures, she will get to dance with the King himself.

And so will you. So don't quit.

The Christian life is really hard—and *really worth it.*

Discussion Questions

1. When the going gets tough, do you "want the tough going to go away"? Why or why not?
2. Is there a time in your life when your faith wavered?
3. Which of the three metaphors that Paul used to describe how we endure can you most identify with—soldier, athlete, or farmer?
4. Have you ever experienced spiritual growth in a time of suffering?
5. How could enduring hardship help you bring other people to Christ?

TAKE ACTION Rate your current endurance level on a scale of 1–10, where 1 is ready to walk off the track and 10 is running strong. Ask God to give you strength to persevere.

7

Protect Your Character

2 Timothy 2:14–26

*"It is not great talent God blesses so much
as great likeness to Jesus. A holy minister is
an awful weapon in the hand of God."*

— ROBERT MURRAY M'CHEYNE

Bible teacher Walter Liefeld tells about a Christian apologist who debated famous atheists like Madeline Murray O'Hair, who sneered at Christian faith. "After one such appearance, some were troubled by this man's combative, demeaning attitude to the antagonist," Liefeld wrote. "The apologist responded to his critics: 'I did not go there to save souls but to destroy a heretic.' I believe the apostle Paul would have hoped rather to destroy heresy and save a soul."[1]

An old proverb says, "Choose your enemies wisely, for you may become them." The proverb is right. When we oppose someone, we risk subtly taking on that person's qualities. If your enemy uses sarcasm, you may become sarcastic yourself. If your enemy exaggerates and conceals, you may begin to rationalize such behavior of your own. If your enemy is insulting and rude, you may begin to act that way too. After all, you're just "fighting fire with fire."

"Choose your enemies wisely, for you may become them."

In 2 Timothy, Paul tells Timothy to confront the false teachers in Ephesus because he is concerned about the dangerous effect of their teaching. But in 2:14–26 specifically, Paul wants to ensure that, in the very act of opposing the false teachers, Timothy will not become like them—that he will be more about saving a soul than destroying a heretic. If he is to finish well someday, Timothy must maintain a distinctly Christian character.

> If he is to finish well, Timothy must maintain a Christian character.

To describe this character, Paul again uses three metaphors. The three metaphors (soldier, athlete, farmer) that Paul uses in 2:1–13 give us pictures for dealing with difficult circumstances. In these next verses, 2:14–26, the three metaphors picture how Timothy should deal with difficult people: with *the integrity of a worker*, *the purity of a noble instrument*, and *the humility of a servant*.

Maintain the Integrity of a Worker

The first metaphor Paul uses is "worker" (2:15). If the church is like a building, then these false teachers are tearing it down, not building it up. In 2:14, when Paul says these false teachers are causing ruin, he uses the Greek word *katastrophe*, a word that could be used for the demolition of a house. These guys are the wrong kind of workmen. In this text, we learn something about the false teachers' *identity, teaching content*, and *effects*.

To begin, we learn their *identity*: Paul mentions Hymenaeus and Philetus by name (2:17). Likely, this is the same Hymenaeus referenced in 1 Timothy 1:20. Notice that they are Greek names—that'll be important in a moment.

Then, we learn the *content* of their teaching. Verse eighteen says they "say that the resurrection has already taken place." Of course, the hope of every Christian is a physical resurrection when Christ returns. In the new heavens and new earth, we'll have a new body. (I personally believe I'll be six foot three, have a full head of hair, and finally be able to dunk a basketball.) In 1 Corinthians 15, Paul says the hope of physical resurrection is at the heart of our faith.

These false teachers, however, deny this hope. Instead, they teach that Christians are spiritually resurrected at baptism, but will never be physically resurrected. *You got a new heart in the past*, they tell believers, *but there is no new body in the future.*

It is certainly true that we're spiritually resurrected at baptism (Rom. 6:4), but why deny the physical resurrection? A prevalent Greek belief was that reality was composed of two substances: the physical and the spiritual. The physical was, by nature, corrupt while the spiritual was, by nature, good. Many, specifically the Stoics (subscribers to the ancient Greek school of philosophy called Stoicism), sought to deny their body because it was inherently evil (see 1 Tim. 4:3). They even used a play on words to summarize their view—*soma sema*, which meant "the body is a tomb."

So the last thing a Greek wanted was to live in a body for all eternity. (Remember that Hymenaeus and Philetus are Greek names.) Apparently, these false teachers had watered down the Christian gospel—compromising to accommodate and even gain approval from their culture. This still happens today:

- To accommodate a culture that values materialism, some preach a "health and wealth" gospel.
- To accommodate a culture that values tolerance over truth, some preach homosexuality as acceptable to God.
- To accommodate a pluralistic culture, some preach Jesus as one way to God, but not the only way to God.

Finally, we learn the *effects* of such false teaching. Paul vividly describes the results. He says it "ruins those who listen" (2:14). "Those who indulge in it will become more and more ungodly" (2:16). It will "spread like gangrene" (2:17). It will "destroy the faith of some" (2:18).

In other words, false teaching is dangerous and destructive. I once heard about a Sunday school teacher who asked her class, "What is false doctrine?" One little boy raised his hand and said, "It's when the doctor gives the wrong stuff to people who are sick." Although the little boy had obviously confused *doctrine* with *doctorin'*, he still arrived at the correct definition. These false teachers were giving out the wrong stuff and endangering people's eternal lives.

To confront these false teachers and "warn them before God" (2:14), Timothy must solemnly charge them to knock it off. In the process, however, he must avoid becoming like the enemy. His opponents play fast and loose with Scripture, but Timothy must maintain his integrity as a "worker who does not need to be ashamed and who correctly handles the word of truth" (2:15).

Paul himself was a worker—a tentmaker by trade (Acts 18:3). Do you think he made sloppy tents? My hunch is that Paul's tents were known for their excellent workmanship (Col. 3:23). Here's an interesting note: the Greek word for "correctly handles" literally means "to cut straight." Paul is telling Timothy to handle the Scripture like Paul handled his leather knife—straight and true.

The call here is for painstaking accuracy when it comes to teaching Scripture. To maintain the integrity of a worker, Timothy must not compromise even a little. We must not be sloppy in studying Scripture. With some things in life, we can settle for "close enough," but other things demand 100 percent accuracy. If 99.9 percent were close enough for maternity wards, then twelve babies would go home every day from the hospital with the wrong parents. Some things you just have to get right.

The Bible is one of those things. God has taken care to communicate with us in words that can be clearly translated, grammatically diagrammed, contextually studied, and personally understood. He chose certain things to say and not say, particular words to use and not use, and we honor God when we pay careful attention to them. Others may be sloppy workers whose careless teaching tears down those around them. We are called to be workers of integrity, building up those around us with careful biblical teaching.

Maintain the Purity of a Noble Instrument

The second metaphor Paul uses is an "instrument"—a household utensil (2:20–21). Every household contains both noble instruments (silver pitcher and fine china) and nasty instruments (slop bucket and toilet plunger). In the same way, the church has both genuine believers and imitation believers. Scripture tells us that on judgment day, God will sort out the good from the bad, the wheat from the weeds, the sheep from the goats (Matt. 13:24–30; 25:31–46).

Timothy may wonder, what if God mistakes him for one of the nasty instruments? Will he fall under God's judgment? Paul reassures Timothy (and the Ephesian church overhearing this letter) with a quotation from Numbers 16:5: "The Lord knows those who are his." Paul describes a figurative picture of an inscription on the foundation stone of the church, alongside another inscription which calls believers to lives of holiness: "Everyone who confesses the name of the Lord must turn away from wickedness" (2:19). Notice that these two inscriptions capture the two sides of salvation—God's and man's. The first is an encouragement, emphasizing God's assurance of salvation; the second is an exhortation, describing our expression of salvation.

While we rest in God's promise, we must still pursue his purity. The false teachers have given themselves over to impurity and wickedness (see 3:1–9). Timothy must not "become like his enemies." Instead of a slop bucket crusted in filth, he must be a clean vessel, a noble instrument for God's use.

> While we rest in God's promise, we must still pursue his purity.

How exactly is Timothy to be a pure instrument for God's use? Paul gives his disciple two strategies. The first strategy is to *run from sin*. Paul writes, "Flee the evil desires of youth" (2:22). A man once came to an old country doctor, saying, "Doc, I broke my arm in two places. What should I do?" The old doctor said, "You ought to stay out of them places!" Paul is charging Timothy to stay out of the places where a spiritual fall might occur.

Because Timothy was a single young man with normal sexual temptations, he probably had to avoid certain streets in Ephesus. The temple of Artemis, the fertility goddess, may have included temple prostitutes, and archaeologists have uncovered—directly across the courtyard from the city library—the Ephesus town brothel. In fact, engravings in the marble street pavement show the way! Timothy is to avoid such places. Like Joseph in Genesis 39, he must run.

This is wise advice, no matter what sin you struggle with. Too many of us make too much provision for temptation for too long. Don't linger in the presence of temptation. As one preacher I heard put it, "If we hesitate, we contemplate. If we contemplate, we negotiate. If we negotiate, we participate. If we participate, we devastate." Too many Christians never make it to the finish line because of moral failure.

Instead, we must flee. The Greek word for "flee" in 2:22 is where we get the English word *fugitive*. We must run like a hunted man from lust, greed, anger, pride, laziness, and every other form of wickedness. As Paul tells Timothy in his first letter, "Run for your life from all this" (1 Tim. 6:11, MSG). The first step to resisting temptation is *removing* temptation.

Removing temptation, however, is not enough. The second step to resisting temptation is *replacing* temptation. Randy Alcorn writes, "Our minds are not vacuums. They will be filled with something. Impure thoughts are pushed out by pure thoughts."[2] The fact is, we must not simply remove evil desire. We must replace it with good (see Matt. 12:43–45). That's why, after Paul says to "flee the evil desires of youth," he says to "pursue righteousness, faith, love and peace" (2:22).

If the first strategy is to run from sin, the second strategy is to *chase after goodness*. Christians are not simply to be known for what we *don't* do—"We don't drink, smoke, chew, or go with girls who do." Ultimately, Christians are to be known for what we *do*—acts of justice and love and peace. Are we actively engaged in developing the character of Jesus? It's not enough to run from the things of the devil; we must also run after the things of Christ.

In fact, the word for "pursue" is most often translated in the New Testament as "persecute." It means *to hunt down with a vengeance.*

Paul is calling Timothy to pursue these character qualities with an intense intentionality—with a vengeance. He mustn't let a day go by without seeking to grow his love and peace and faith, without adding to their muscle, without checking to see if he is making progress.

Do you check your spiritual progress? When I was a kid, my dad would mark my height on the basement wall. Each year I could visibly see my growth. If there was a spiritual growth chart on your wall, would you have grown at all since last year? How intentional are you about your spiritual development?

We must constantly evaluate where we need to grow in Christ: Is it in developing loving relationships, or exercising gentleness, or being marked by joy, or practicing self-control? And then we must actively engage in growing. If I'm not a person of joy, for example, then I should strategize ways to grow in joy:

- Memorize Scriptures about joy.
- Hang around children—they are so good at joy.
- Make time in my schedule to slow down and enjoy God's creation.
- Learn a new joke and tell it three times this week.
- Sing.
- Pray that God will infect me with his joy.

This is what the active pursuit of righteousness looks like. Be intentional. As you cultivate your likeness to Jesus, you, like Timothy, will be a noble instrument for God's use, "an awful weapon in the hand of God."

Maintain the Humility of a Servant

The false teachers Timothy must face are proud and full of hot air, and they attack the young man with criticism. I once heard an oft-repeated story about evangelist Dwight L. Moody. Moody received a note containing a single word: "Fool." Moody said he'd received many critical letters where the writers left their name off, but this was the first time a writer had left off the message and signed his name!

It would be easy for Timothy to attack these false teachers back. But Paul tells Timothy he must not become like his enemies by retaliating. In 2:24, Paul says that he ought to respond by being "kind"—the same word Paul used to describe a nurse taking care of her children (1 Thess. 2:7). Timothy must maintain a spirit that is "not resentful"—which could be translated "patient with difficult people" (NLT).

In fact, the last metaphor Paul uses to describe Timothy's character is a "servant," or more accurately, a slave. The Greek word is *doulos*—the "lowest term in the scale of servitude."[3] Specifically, Paul calls Timothy "the Lord's *doulos*." This metaphor serves as a reminder of two important truths: Timothy is not as important as what he might be tempted to think, and God is the one who will ultimately defend him, since he belongs to the Lord.

These reminders are incredibly freeing. While the false teachers' pride expressed itself in arrogant argument and defensive quarrels, Timothy could be free from such things. Instead, he could "gently" instruct, "in the hope that God will grant them repentance leading them to a knowledge of the truth" (2:25). Timothy can offer correction in a non-angry, non-defensive, humble spirit.

When we seek to correct wrong teaching, we are to manifest humility and grace, not arrogance and hostility. Author Karl Vaters notes that a growing number of Christians on social media post memes or videos with headlines like: "Student Humiliates Atheist Professors Who Tried to Tell Him God Isn't Real!" or, "A Simple Illustration That Destroys (insert counterargument here)!" or, "Mormons Get Schooled by Christian Man!"[4] Such hostile approaches alienate those who oppose us.

What difference could a gracious and humble approach make? Ken Parker was a white supremacist, a self-proclaimed Nazi and grand dragon in the KKK. In 2017, Ken and his fiancée saw a black man—Pastor William McKinnon—cooking out by their apartment complex pool, and though Ken's body bore tattoos of swastikas, Confederate flags, and the words "white pride," Pastor McKinnon invited them to eat with him.

Over the next weeks, a friendship began to grow. McKinnon didn't attack them or seek to "destroy" their wrong thinking. He invited Ken and his fiancée to his all-black church, where they were greeted with the love of Christ. "After the service, they were all coming up and hugging me," said Ken later, "building me up instead of tearing me down." Many conversations followed about Ken's beliefs, and in 2018, Pastor McKinnon led Ken in his baptismal robe into the Atlantic Ocean, baptizing him into Christ. "How are you feeling now?" someone asked him. The former KKK member answered, "Better than the last time I had a robe on."[5]

An old proverb reminds us, "Once you've cut off a person's nose, there's no point giving him a rose to smell." If we are harsh to those who oppose us, they'll tune us out when we offer them the gospel. We must be bold enough to correct wrong-headed beliefs, but gentle enough to encourage a hearing when we speak of Jesus.

One last reminder when confronting: remember who the real enemy is. It's true that when confronting these false teachers, Timothy must not "become like his enemies." But the fact is that the real enemy is Satan. In 2:26, Paul says that Timothy's opponents have actually been taken captive by the devil. Though they oppose the true gospel, at the end of the day they are prisoners of war, not enemies. They are victims of our real nemesis. When we remember this, we will seek not simply to win the argument but to win their souls.

As we maintain the integrity of a worker, the purity of an instrument, and the humility of a servant, may we see our enemies return to the side of God.

Discussion Questions

1. Rate your Bible knowledge on a scale of 1–10, 10 being an expert and 1 being a novice. How well could you tell the difference between Bible and "almost Bible"?
2. What are two to three things you could do to become a better Bible student?
3. Paul told Timothy to run for his life from temptation. What makes this difficult in our culture?
4. Paul also tells Timothy to "pursue righteousness with a vengeance." What are some specific ways you could follow Paul's command?
5. Have you ever had to correct someone's wrong understanding? How did it make you feel?

TAKE ACTION Ask God to build your character and begin to make it a habit in your prayers.

8

Choose Wise Examples

2 Timothy 3:1–13

*"Example is not the main thing in
influencing others. It is the only thing."*

— ALBERT SCHWEITZER

Ethel sat beside her dying husband's bed. "Ethel," Ray said, "You've always been by my side. When we were poor newlyweds, you were there. When I broke my leg, you were there. When I lost my job in '72, you were there. When the fire destroyed our house in '87, you were there. Do you remember when I was in the car wreck? You were there. No matter what difficulty came our way, you were always there."

Ray looked up at his wife with tears in his eyes. "You know something, Ethel? You're bad luck!"

Being around certain people is bad for you.

I once heard a preacher say we have two kinds of relationships: balcony people and basement people.[1] Balcony people lift us up—cheering us on and calling forth our best. Basement people, on the other hand, drag us down. They infect us with a negative attitude, discouraging us and leading us down the low road.

This is why Scripture is clear that we are to guard our close associations—the people we spend time with whom we allow to speak into our lives. Look at 1 Corinthians 15:33: "Do not be misled: 'Bad company corrupts good character.'" Notice that before Paul tells Timothy to fill himself with the Good Book (2 Tim. 3:14–17), he tells him to surround himself with good *people* (3:1–13).

Avoiding Dangerous Examples

Paul begins this passage in 2 Timothy 3:1–13 by warning Timothy of what we might call "basement people." By the way, don't let the phrase "in the last days" fool you (3:1). Paul isn't pointing to some future era. In the New Testament, "the last days" began the moment that Christ was born in Bethlehem. Both Acts 2:14–17 and Hebrews 1:1–2 make clear that "the last days" arrived with the first coming of Christ. The final era of history has begun. We are living in the last days, as was Timothy.

So the warning Paul gives here is not for the future, but for the present. In 3:1–9, Paul paints a picture of the false teachers that serves as a wanted poster. In fact, the Greek word "terrible" in 3:1 could be translated "dangerous." It's used elsewhere to describe wild animals, wild seas, and wild human beings, like the demon-possessed men in Matthew 8:28. The false teachers Paul will describe, then, are not just annoyances; they are threats. They pose a great danger to Timothy's spiritual health, as well as that of the Ephesian church.

The problem, of course, is that these false teachers can be hard to identify. They don't wear black hats or name tags that say "Heretic." They don't stand up during Sunday morning announcements and say, "We're beginning a small group tonight where our teaching will lead you into the trap of the devil, who will take you captive to do his will. You can sign up out in the church lobby on the clipboard marked 'False Teacher Fellowship Group.'"

Instead, the teachers in this passage appear very likable. They're knowledgeable, charismatic, and persuasive. In fact, they have already won the confidence of several women in the congregation (see 3:6). So how can Timothy distinguish genuine sheep from wolves in sheep's clothing (Matt. 7:15)? The vice list in 3:2–4 acts as a police sketch artist's drawing of the suspects. Timothy must keep his eyes open for those who match this description.

The list of vices includes nineteen character traits, and the first and last traits intentionally serve as bookends. The other seventeen traits fall between and are a result of these two characteristics: "lovers of themselves . . . rather than lovers of God" (3:2, 4). The proper order, of course, is to love God first, neighbor second, and self last. But these false teachers in Ephesus swapped the first and third places. When we put self first and God last, our neighbor in the middle is bound to suffer. In fact, the other seventeen vices that Paul lists are almost entirely about the false teachers' mistreatment of those around them.

As we study these vices, we want to make two evaluations. First, evaluate yourself. Do you see these characteristics in your own life? All of us are capable of these vices, so look at this sketch and then look in the mirror. Guard your heart from the insidious increeping of sin.

Second, evaluate your close associations. Do you see these characteristics in your friends and influencers? Think also of your media intake—TV, movies, music, internet. Some people know their favorite sitcom characters better than they know their neighbors. Do these vices describe the musicians, talk show hosts, or movie characters you admire? The Bible clearly labels some people as evil. We are to avoid them because they have fallen so deeply into sinful habits that they are now "men of depraved minds, who, as far as the faith is concerned, are rejected" (3:8). If we're not careful, these "basement people" will drag us down with them.

Who's Your Role Model?

To help you make these evaluations, I have summarized Paul's list of vices with six questions you can ask yourself about the people you associate with closely:

1. *Do they focus more on themselves or others?* Paul says the false teachers are "lovers of themselves," "boastful," and "proud." Pay attention to those who influence you: Do they show genuine interest in others or focus on themselves? In the nineteenth century, two of Britain's greatest politicians were William Gladstone and Benjamin

Disraeli. It was said that when you dined with Gladstone, you thought you were *with* the world's most brilliant conversationalist. But when you dined with Disraeli—who could be equally as charming—he made you feel like *you* were the world's most brilliant conversationalist. Who are your friends more like—Gladstone or Disraeli?

2. *Are they preoccupied with money or things?* Ephesus was an affluent city, the commercial center of Asia Minor. Money flowed like water. Like contemporary Americans, Timothy could easily have succumbed to the materialistic, consumer culture surrounding him. Apparently the false teachers already had, because Paul calls them "lovers of money" and "lovers of pleasure." Ask yourself: Are my role models focused on salary, house, car, clothes, boat, tech toys, or stuff? Or do they live for more eternal interests?

3. *Do they treat others with kindness or rudeness/sarcasm?* Paul uses words like "abusive," "disobedient to their parents," and "slanderous" to describe these men. Do those around you speak against others unkindly? Do their attitudes reveal a callousness toward others' feelings? Do they speak disrespectfully to or about authority figures such as parents or bosses? Just as a doctor asks his patient to stick out their tongue and say "Ahh," we can check the spiritual health of those around us by paying attention to their tongues.

4. *How would you describe their attitude—entitled or grateful?* The Roman philosopher Cicero said that gratitude is the parent of all virtues. When a person exhibits thankfulness, they show that they are someone who appreciates others' contributions. That "others-awareness" can grow into kindness, patience, and other virtues. But the absence of gratitude signals a person who believes that people exist for their benefit, and such self-centeredness can grow into the other vices Paul mentions here. That's why "ungrateful" is smack dab in the middle of the list.

5. *Do they have a quick temper or act without thinking?* Paul says these false teachers were "without self-control" and "rash." People like this can't control their impulses or their emotions. Proverbs 22:24–25

tells us, "Do not make friends with a hot-tempered person . . . or you may learn their ways."

6. *Does their life show that they truly love God?* Do you surround yourself with people who speak of God, read his Word, pray, give their time or money to kingdom causes, obey scriptural commands, and exhibit the fruit of the Spirit? If you have a hard time detecting these values in the people you spend time with, they may fall under Paul's labels of "unholy" and not "lovers of God."

The Power of a Poor Example

The bottom line is that these false teachers are hypocrites. Second Timothy 3:5 says they are displaying "a form of godliness but denying its power." In other words, they're all show and no substance; all talk and no walk—imitations, not the real thing.

At an annual meeting of the American Heart Association, one blogger reported how 300,000 doctors, nurses, and medical professionals met in Atlanta to discuss important topics, one of which was the importance of a low-fat diet. "Yet during mealtimes, they consumed fat-filled fast foods such as bacon cheeseburgers and fries at the same rate as people from other conventions. When one cardiologist was asked . . . [if] his high-fat meals set a bad example, he replied, 'Not me, because I took my name tag off.'"[2]

The false teachers had the same flawed thinking: as long as I say the right things, I don't have to do the right things. They were "always learning but never able to come to a knowledge of the truth" (3:7). They read the Bible for information, but not for transformation. They may have known lots of biblical facts, but they didn't live biblically. If your leaders know ten times more Bible than anyone else but are zero times more joyful, loving, faithful, and self-controlled, watch out! I like what Bible commentator Matthew Henry said: "Those who teach by their doctrine must teach by their live [*sic*], else they pull down with one hand what they build up with the other."[3]

Paul knew the destructive influence the false teachers' example would have on their followers. As Proverbs 13:20 puts it, "Whoever walks with the wise becomes wise, but the companion of fools will suffer harm." A preacher I heard once shared this proverb: "What you do speaks so loudly that I cannot hear what you are saying," and the false teachers' lifestyle was speaking the wrong message. The apostle did not want their lives to rub off on Timothy or the Ephesian church.

Baseball player Billy Martin once told a story about hunting in Texas with Mickey Mantle. They drove to the ranch of one of Mantle's friends, and Mickey went inside to ask permission to hunt. Mantle's friend quickly gave permission but asked a favor: Would Mickey go out to the barn and put down an old mule that was going blind?

Mickey decided to have a little fun with Billy. When Mickey returned to the car, he pretended to be angry. Slamming the door, Mickey said his friend wouldn't let them hunt: "I'm so mad at that guy. I'm going out to his barn and shooting one of his mules!" Mantle drove like a crazy man to the barn. Martin protested, "We can't do that!" But Mickey shouted, "Just watch me," jumped out of the car with his rifle, ran inside, and shot the mule.

As he was leaving, though, he heard two shots, and he ran back to the car. He saw that Martin had pulled out his rifle too. "What are you doing, Martin?" Mantle yelled. Martin yelled back, face red with anger, "We'll show that son of a gun! I just killed two of his cows!"[4]

It's not just anger that can be contagious. Any vice can begin to spread like an infectious disease. Paul gives Timothy one instruction about these bad examples: avoid them.

This does not mean Timothy is to treat them with a judgmental or superior attitude. Nor does it mean Timothy is to be an isolationist who avoids all contact with non-Christians. (How could we influence them for Christ?) First Corinthians 5:9–11 tells us to avoid immoral people in the *church*, not in the *world*.

Rather, Timothy is to avoid these false teachers to protect his own soul. He is to stay out from under their influence. Paul says they are like Jannes and Jambres, traditionally the names given to Pharaoh's magicians who opposed Moses (Exod. 7–9). The false teachers are imposters like those magicians were; they too stand in opposition to

God, their judgment is coming, and Timothy won't want to be caught in the fallout.

We too must carefully evaluate the people we allow to influence us. An ancient Greek proverb says, "A people are known by the heroes they crown." Who are your role models, your examples? Whose priorities, beliefs, and habits tend to rub off on you? Paul tells Timothy, and us, to steadfastly avoid those who will lead us away from God. God will judge those whose faith is not genuine, and you don't want to be caught in the fallout.

> We must carefully evaluate the people we allow to influence us.

Remember Ray and Ethel: being around certain people is bad for you.

Choosing Wise Examples

On the other hand, being around certain people is good for you.

In 3:10, Paul turns from negative examples to a positive example—himself. While the apostle certainly knew his own sinfulness (1 Tim. 1:15), he also pursued Christ so fervently that he often called others to follow in his footsteps (see 1 Thess. 1:6; 2 Thess. 3:7, 9; 1 Cor. 4:6; 11:1; Phil. 3:17; and 4:9). If the false teachers were imitation Christianity, then Paul was Christianity worth imitating. His life was a kind of living Bible for others to read.

Timothy had clearly taken Paul as his role model. The word for "you know" in 3:10 is a strong Greek word, *parakolouthein*, which means to follow physically, mentally, and spiritually. William Barclay writes, "*Parakolouthein* is indeed the word for the disciple, for it includes the unwavering loyalty of the true comrade, the understanding of the true student and the obedience of the dedicated servant."[5] Timothy had lived with, looked at, and learned from the great apostle.

In contrast to the false teachers, Paul offers a virtue list from his own life as a pattern that Timothy can follow. Unlike the hypocritical teachers, Paul was the real deal. His conduct matched his creed, and he was the same man in the marketplace as in the church, in hard times as in good times. Let's look at what Timothy saw lived out in his mentor:

- *His purpose.* Paul lived for one thing alone: to know Christ and to make him known (Phil. 1:21).
- *His faith.* When it looked foolish to human eyes, Paul still trusted completely in God's promises.
- *His patience.* Timothy watched as Paul refused to get irritated with frustrating people and circumstances. Paul kept his head.
- *His love.* Paul did not treat people as objects, projects, or a means to an end. He genuinely cared for them as a father does his children (1 Thess. 2:11).
- *His endurance.* Certainly Timothy had witnessed the persecution the apostle had suffered. In fact, Timothy was from Lystra (3:11), where he may have seen Paul stoned and left for dead (Acts 14). Yet Paul wouldn't quit preaching the gospel.

Paul wants this list to stir Timothy's courage, to inspire him to follow the example he has set. He wants Timothy to display the same virtues. And Paul especially wants his own finish-line faith to rub off on Timothy. An ounce of example is worth a pound of preaching, so Paul points to his life and says, *If I can endure hunger, cold, loneliness, beating, flogging, stoning, and near death, you can surely endure the challenges of a difficult ministry.*

When New Testament scholar William Lane taught at Western Kentucky University, one of his students was contemporary Christian musician Michael Card. They developed a friendship that led to a discipling relationship, and Michael learned how to read Scripture, how to treat his wife, how to serve the church, and how to love God by watching Dr. Lane. Eventually Michael graduated, Dr. Lane moved to another university, and though they stayed in touch, their lives took separate paths.

Years later, Professor Lane was diagnosed with terminal cancer, and the Lanes decided to move to Franklin, Tennessee, where Michael

Card lived with his family. As Card tells the story, Professor Lane had a purpose in this. He said to Michael on the phone, "I want to come to Franklin . . . I want to show you how a Christian man dies." The Lanes made the move, and many months later Card's beloved mentor died. But he left behind a powerful lesson in finishing well.[6]

That's what Paul has done for Timothy. Now Timothy must live what he has seen. Timothy will most certainly experience difficult times (3:12), but if he perseveres like Paul, the Lord will rescue him as well (3:11).

The Power of a Positive Example

Now I want you to ask yourself two questions:

First, *Do I have someone in my life I can look to? Am I following in their footsteps?* Abraham Heschel wrote, "What we need more than anything else is not textbooks but text-people. It is the personality of the teacher which is the text that the pupils read; the text they will never forget."[7]

Growing up, I watched my dad. I watched when he began every morning with his open Bible on his lap. I watched when he walked in the door every evening and his first order of business was kissing my mom. I watched when my corporate executive dad picked up the mentally handicapped guys from the county home for church and treated them with as much dignity as he would the company president. An African proverb says, "A good example is the tallest kind of preaching," and my dad's life is a sermon I'll never forget.

We all need those examples in our lives, so keep your eyes open. It may be a parent or grandparent, a leader in your church, someone in your small group, or even someone whose life you've read about in church history. Don't put these people on a pedestal. But if they're truly following Christ, you can learn by following them.

The second question to consider is this: *Am I someone other people can look to? Do others want to follow in my footsteps?* We are called to live in such a way that we can say, as Paul writes, "Follow my example, as I follow the example of Christ" (1 Cor. 11:1). Can you say to others,

"Drive as I drive, spend money as I spend money, watch TV as I watch TV, love your spouse as I love my spouse, serve as I serve, speak as I speak, think as I think, and walk as I walk"?

> **If you want finish-line faith, choose wise examples.**

If you want finish-line faith, choose wise examples. If you want those around you to have finish-line faith, be a wise example.

Remember Ray and Ethel? May you live in such a way that someday someone says, "Being around you was good for me."

Discussion Questions

1. Which one of the six evaluation questions was most convicting to you?
2. What media or influences in your life do you need to reevaluate?
3. Why do we sometimes enjoy influences like this even when we know it's not helping our holiness?
4. Name some positive examples in your life. Whose life has inspired or influenced you?
5. Who is watching *your* example?

TAKE ACTION Take time to thank God for the positive examples in your life.

9

Nourish Yourself on Scripture

2 Timothy 3:14–17

"A Bible that is falling apart usually belongs to someone whose life isn't."

— CHARLES SPURGEON

Y ou are what you eat.

Physically, this proverb is true. If all you eat are carrots, you'll be as skinny and as orange as a carrot. If all you eat are Big Macs, you'll look like a Big Mac. Spiritually, this proverb rings even truer. What you feed your mind and soul will shape who you become.

True story: A young Austrian teenager wanted desperately to be an artist, but his application to the prestigious Vienna art school was sent back twice with the words "drawings unsatisfactory" scrawled across the top. Stung by the rejection, he did what many teenagers do—he withdrew into his own world. Isolated in his room, he devoured the writings of German philosopher Friedrich Nietzsche, who taught that God was dead and that the purpose of life was to gain power. He immersed himself in the music of Richard Wagner, whose anti-Semitism and rabid Germanic nationalism bled freely into his compositions. Of course, those books and that music profoundly shaped that young man—whose name was Adolf Hitler—and shaped the course of world history.

You are what you eat.

The Shaping Power of Your Mental Diet

The music, television, books, conversations, movies, and websites you constantly expose yourself to will mold your character. An old proverb says, "Sow a thought; reap a deed. Sow a deed; reap a habit. Sow a habit; reap a character. Sow a character; reap a destiny." Notice that it all starts with a thought. "As he thinketh in his heart, so is he" (Prov. 23:7, KJV). What you put into your mind will determine who you become. You are what you eat.

That's why Scripture uses the image of eating as a metaphor for Bible intake:

- "Then he said to me, 'Son of man, eat this scroll I am giving you and fill your stomach with it.' So I ate it, and it tasted as sweet as honey in my mouth" (Ezek. 3:3).
- "How sweet are your words to my taste, sweeter than honey to my mouth" (Ps. 119:103).
- "When your words came, I ate them; they were my joy and my heart's delight" (Jer. 15:16).
- God's Word is compared to milk, bread, and meat (1 Pet. 2:2; Deut. 8:3; Heb. 5:12).

We are to feed ourselves on the Word of Christ so that we can be transformed into the likeness of Christ. In 1 Timothy 4:6, Paul uses this metaphor when he tells Timothy that a good minister of Christ Jesus is "nourished on the truths of the faith." Timothy is to nourish himself with Scripture.

In 2 Timothy 3:14–17, Paul returns to this theme. As Timothy faces off against dangerous foes (3:1–9), he can draw strength from God's Word. The words of the Bible will get into his marrow, course through his veins, and metabolize into new energy, courage, and power. God's Word will give him finish-line faith.

Paul says that Timothy "from infancy" has "known the Holy Scriptures" (3:15). The Jewish people took the biblical education of their children seriously. At age six, Jewish boys would start school at the village synagogue, and as one ancient Jewish rabbi said, "We take a child and stuff him with Torah [Old Testament Scriptures] like an ox." While the half-Gentile Timothy might not have attended synagogue school, his Jewish mother and grandmother fed him generous helpings of God's Word from his earliest days.

But perhaps recently he had lost his hunger for Scripture. We know that Paul tells Timothy not to abandon the Scriptures. "Continue" in them, he says. "Abide in them, live in them, immerse yourself in them."

I read about an Ethiopian king named Menelik II who took the eating metaphor literally. Whenever he became sick, he would tear pages from the Bible and swallow them in the mistaken belief that this would cure him. He died in 1913 after devouring all of 2 Kings!

When I first read that story, I chuckled. Well, he took this eating imagery a little too seriously, didn't he? But then the Holy Spirit pricked my conscience: Do I take this metaphor seriously enough? Jesus said, "Man shall not live on bread alone, but on every word that comes from the mouth of God" (Matt. 4:4). Is that true of me? Do I need God's Word to *live*?

Evaluate yourself. Would you feel hunger pangs if you went without reading your Bible? Can you truly say, as Job did in Job 23:12, "I have treasured the words of his mouth more than my daily bread"?

Perhaps you have lost your hunger, and you too need to hear the reasons Paul gives Timothy to "continue" in the Scriptures (3:14). Paul mentions three reasons Scripture nourishes us: because it's *from God*, it's *about Christ*, and it's *for us*.

Scripture Nourishes Because It's from God

Timothy must nourish himself on Scripture because these words come to us straight from God. They are "God-breathed"—so fresh from his mouth you can still catch the scent of his breath on the pages. The Bible is like no other book. All other literature originates on this planet, but the Bible comes to us from outside our sphere of existence. It is literally from heaven.

The unity of these authors—some forty writers on three continents in three different languages over the course of 1,500 years all telling the same story—points to Scripture's divine origin.

The humanity of these authors points to God's relational purpose. God stooped to speak to us through people like us—in understandable human language—so he could establish relationship with us. He could have remained above human contact, inscrutable, unreachable. But as Carl Henry said, the Bible is "God's free and gracious choice to give up his privacy that we may know Him."[1]

Through Scripture, God allows us to get inside his head, read his mail, eavesdrop on his heavenly council chamber, see the world through his eyes, and hear his most personal thoughts. Such behind-the-scenes access to the Creator of the universe is nothing less than an invitation to *know* him.

> Through Scripture, God allows us to hear his personal thoughts.

This realization can stir a hunger for God's Word. Some time ago, my wife, Katie, and I were rummaging through an attic box of old college keepsakes. I reached for a large manila envelope, wondering what was inside. Old love letters! I pulled out a thick stack of envelopes Katie had sent me one summer when we were dating.

We were apart all summer, and I remember waiting eagerly for those twice-a-week letters in the mail. I would tear open the envelope and devour every sentence—reading and rereading every word, imagining the voice of my beloved speaking them to me. The letter read "Dear Matt," but behind the words I could hear her heart's true message—"my handsome hunk of a guy." Those letters were my lifeline to her. I could almost quote them because I lingered over them so long.

(By the way, Katie pulled out of the manila envelope *both* of the letters I wrote her that summer. I'm a communication slob.)

Why did I read these letters so hungrily? Because they were from someone I loved—someone who also loved me. Remember: the Bible is a personal letter to you from the Lover of your soul. He wrote it because he wants a relationship with you. We are to read this book because it is *from God.*

Scripture Nourishes Because It's About Christ

The Scriptures point to Jesus. This is the second reason why Timothy must nourish himself on God's Word. Paul reminds him that the Scriptures "are able to make you wise for salvation through faith in Christ Jesus" (3:15). At this point Timothy only had the Old Testament, but those thirty-nine books were written to predict, prepare for, and describe the coming Messiah. In John 5:39 Jesus said, "The very Scriptures . . . testify about me." In Luke 24:27 the resurrected Christ took the Emmaus travelers on a journey through the entire Bible, explaining to them "what was said in all the Scriptures concerning himself."

The Bible was written to reveal Christ. It is wonderfully diverse, but Jesus taught that all the stories and statutes, prophecies and proclamations, lists and laments, proverbs and prayers somehow found their focus in him. Scholar Norman Geisler put it this way:

- In the Old Testament Law, we find the foundation for Christ.
- In the Old Testament books of history, we find the preparation for Christ.
- In the Old Testament books of poetry, we find the aspiration for Christ.
- In the Old Testament Prophets, we find the expectation of Christ.
- In the New Testament Gospels, we find the manifestation of Christ.
- In Acts, we find the propagation of Christ.
- In the Epistles, we find the interpretation of Christ.
- In Revelation, we find the consummation in Christ.[2]

When someone wants to find Jesus, the best place to look is in the Bible.

As a children's church teacher, I'm often asked to talk with children who are considering baptism. After attending church with a friend, a little girl named Tesslah decided she wanted to be baptized. I called her unchurched parents to ask if they would come to our church building on a Tuesday evening as I discussed baptism with their daughter. They agreed, listening in that evening as I explained to Tesslah what giving her life to Jesus meant.

They came the next Sunday when I baptized Tesslah, and I noticed that her mother, Karen, came back the following Sunday . . . and the following Sunday. After three weeks, Karen approached me with one of our church's free "take one if you want one" Bibles in her hand. She said simply, "I've been reading this for three weeks, and I'm ready." In the pages of Scripture, she had come face-to-face with Jesus, and now she wanted to follow him.

Not only do the Scriptures lead us to initial faith in Jesus; after we become disciples, they continue to strengthen our faith in him. Simply put, your soul's health is measured by this one test: How well do you know Christ? If he is your "friend who sticks closer than a brother," your "rock and redeemer," the "desire of your heart," then regardless of trials, you will find spiritual energy coursing through your veins.

But if you think little of Christ, are content to live without awareness of his presence, care little for his concerns, then you will find your soul weary and weak.

How then can you grow in your love and knowledge of Christ? Read his Word. When you open the pages of Scripture, you will find yourself following along the dusty roads after the Galilean rabbi—hearing his voice, seeing his smile, watching his interactions with people like the ones you know, noticing the tiny moments of compassion that reveal his character, absorbing his passion for truth, listening to him pray, and sharing in his life.

We are to nourish ourselves on the Scriptures because they are *about Christ*.

Scripture Nourishes Because It's for Us

What I mean is, they are for our good. The Scriptures teach us how to live "the life you've always wanted."[3] One preacher said it well: "A Bible that is falling apart usually belongs to someone whose life isn't."[4] In 3:16, Paul tells Timothy that Scripture is useful for:

- Teaching: *telling us what's right*
- Rebuking: *telling us what's not right*
- Correcting: *telling us how to get right*
- Training in righteousness: *telling us how to stay right*[5]

I'm confident that anyone who reads the Bible regularly will find that, over time, their lives are transformed. Bible reading is not like drinking caffeine—that instant jolt to get you through the next few hours. It's more like taking vitamins—strengthening you with greater health over the long haul. As we meditate on Scripture, we slowly become people marked by goodness, joy, courage, patience, and wisdom. When you pick up a Bible, you're not just holding twelve ounces of paper, ink, and glue. You're holding the possibility of a whole new life.

> Bible reading is like taking vitamins—strengthening you over the long haul.

Yet I wonder if we often opt to pick up the latest devotional book instead of our Bible. I am often asked for book recommendations: *Do you know of a good book on parenting or marriage or money management?* I'm grateful for the Christian books on my shelf, but I always try to point people to Scripture first for the help they need.

- Want to sharpen your leadership? Read Nehemiah.
- Looking for money management advice? Read Proverbs.
- Exploring the meaning of life? Read Ecclesiastes.
- Dealing with a difficult boss? Read Daniel.
- Need to know how to romance your spouse? Read Song of Songs.

- Want guidance on deepening your prayer life? Read Psalms.
- Trying to find joy in trials? Read Philippians.

You have an entire Christian bookstore between the covers of your Bible. Don't settle for good books without reading the best Book. Only God's Word is "alive and active. Sharper than any double-edged sword" (Heb. 4:12). Only God's Word has the power to transform our lives. My friend Joe Puentes once told me that in his Hispanic community they have a saying: *Ha sido tan buena la Biblia con nosotros* (The Bible has been very good to us).

We nourish ourselves on Scripture because it's from God, about Christ, and *for us.*

Three Strategies for Scriptural Nourishment

To close this chapter, I'd like to suggest some practical application for how you can take God's Word into your life.

1. *Get it in your hand.* Here, I'm referring to regular Bible reading. In a Barna survey, almost 90 percent of Americans said they do not read the Bible daily.[6] We're facing what Amos 8:11 calls "a famine of . . . the words of the LORD." Here in the United States, we have greater access to the Word of God than any people in history—available online and in dozens of printed translations. The banquet table is set, but we're starving ourselves.

Schedule a standing appointment with God in his Word. Find a regular place and a Bible reading plan to help you read God's Word intelligently, systematically. Then make Bible reading a daily habit.

A billboard sponsored by the Cattlemen's Association read, "Eat beef. The West wasn't won on salad." You won't develop finish-line faith by nibbling. Dive into the meat and potatoes of God's Word. Nourish yourself on Scripture.

2. *Get it in your heart.* I'm talking about meditating on God's Word. Psalm 1:2 says the man of God "meditates on his law day and night." While Eastern meditation seeks to *empty* the mind, biblical meditation seeks to *fill* the mind with God's truth. How? By devoting time and reflection. Rather than one big gulp of Bible reading,

meditation chews Scripture slowly. This kind of reader "does not always remain bent over his pages; he often leans back and closes his eyes over a line he has been reading again" and its meaning enters his soul as food enters his stomach.[7] This must be done slowly; you can speed read, but you cannot speed meditate.

What exactly does this meditation look like? Like a dog gnawing on a bone—turn a verse or phrase over and over in your mind and pray through it. Savor every word, allowing all of its nutrients to absorb into your mind and heart. Rewrite the text in your own words. Internalize it, because as Dallas Willard reminds us, "It is better in one year to have ten good verses transferred *into the substance of our lives* than to have every word of the Bible flash before our eyes."[8]

3. *Get it in your head.* Yes, I'm talking about Bible memorization. The purpose of memorizing Scripture is to have it ready when the Holy Spirit needs it. The Holy Spirit wants to sculpt us into the image of Christ, and the primary tools he uses are the Scriptures we've stored in our minds. But too often, he goes to our mental toolbox, and all he finds is a John 3:16. We haven't given him much to work with.

If you can remember your Social Security number, your kids' names, and the words to "Jesus Loves Me," then you can memorize Scripture. So pick one verse a week. Say it over and over. Meditate on it. Write it on an index card and carry it with you. Pull it out when you have three minutes during the day to review. Stick it on your mirror as you get ready in the morning. Make it your phone screen. Practice writing it out from memory. Find a partner to help you memorize it.

As a missionary to China, J. Russell Morse was arrested in the 1940s for preaching Christ. He spent fifteen months in a Chinese Communist prison. Telling the story of Morse, Seth Wilson wrote, "He endured severe tortures and terrific strain supported chiefly by his memory of the Bible. He testifies that the promises and precepts of God's Word came to him in memory and gave strength, wisdom and hope which were sorely needed. That's why he urges all his brethren to fill their memories with that living and powerful Word."[9]

As Paul himself languishes in prison, he knows his own need to gather strength from Scripture. In 2 Timothy 4:13, he asks Timothy to come visit him quickly, bringing with him "the parchments." Most scholars agree: Paul is asking for his copies of the Old Testament Scriptures. He was arrested so suddenly that he wasn't able to grab his Bible, but now he wants to read it in his prison cell. After a lifetime of study (I'll bet Paul's Bible was well-worn), he still wanted to read it again.

What a powerful example for Timothy! Paul finished well because he was, in John Wesley's words, "a man of one book."[10] He filled his life with God's Word, and in the process became God's man. Now Timothy must become such a man, so he must nourish himself on the Scriptures.

After all, you are what you eat.

Discussion Questions

1. If the Bible were a food, what food would it be? Salad? Chocolate? Steak? Why?
2. What do you think God wanted to accomplish by giving us his words in the Scriptures?
3. How has your Bible reading grown your relationship with him?
4. Share a time when learning biblical truths or principles helped you in a practical way.
5. Rate your consistency in Bible reading on a scale of 1–10, with 1 being never and 10 being every day. Do you meditate on or memorize Scripture?

TAKE ACTION Choose a Bible verse this week to memorize. Thank God for the wonderful gift of his Word.

10

Speak God's Message

2 Timothy 4:1–8

"Every Christian is either a missionary or an imposter."

— CHARLES SPURGEON

Some are noble. As the British prepared to hang Nathan Hale as a Revolutionary War spy, he uttered these famous words: "I only regret that I have but one life to give for my country."

Some are tender. On his deathbed, President James Polk whispered to his wife, "I love you, Sarah. For all eternity, I love you."

Some are despairing. As she lay dying, Queen Elizabeth I wished for an impossible trade: "All my possessions for a moment of time."

Some are downright cranky. The final recorded words of author H. G. Wells were spoken to a nurse: "Go away! I'm alright."

Last words are many things, but the one thing last words are *not* is ignored. Shakespeare wrote, "The tongues of dying men enforce attention like deep harmony."[1] When a man is on his deathbed, those around him lean in to listen well.

As Timothy nears the end of this letter, he knows he may be reading the apostle's last words. Timothy knows Paul is imprisoned in Rome on death row. He knows that winter will soon shut down any ocean travel, that he may not make it to Rome before Paul is executed. Timothy knows the parchment he holds in his hands may be his mentor's final letter.

I can see Timothy leaning in to read these last lines. Paul will not waste his last breath; he will not spill his final ink carelessly. What beats most strongly in Paul's heart in this, his last hour? What charge does Paul most want to leave echoing in Timothy's mind?

"In the presence of God and of Christ, who will judge the living and the dead, and in view of his appearing and his kingdom, I give you this charge: Preach the word" (4:1–2).

Paul's last words are as simple as they are compelling: *Preach the Word.* The Greek word for "preach" simply means to speak a message on behalf of the king. Paul is calling Timothy to speak God's message, to tell others about Christ. Timothy must give himself to the work of evangelism. Paul's last command is the same as Christ's last mandate in Matthew 28:19–20: "Go and make disciples of all nations, baptizing them . . . and teaching them."

This preaching is not restricted to those who occupy pulpits. In Mark 1:45, the healed leper went about "preaching" the good news of what Jesus had done for him—the same word used in 2 Timothy 4:2. All of us who have experienced Jesus' healing touch are called to "preach."

We have all been charged to spread the message of Jesus Christ. I still remember hearing one woman talk about her work: "I'm a missionary . . . cleverly disguised as a grocery store clerk." Every Christian is called to be a missionary, a preacher cleverly disguised as a teacher, truck driver, or accountant. In this text, Paul mentions three reasons why Timothy must speak God's message: because *Jesus is coming, Satan is deceiving,* and *Paul is leaving.*

> We have all been charged to spread the message of Jesus Christ.

Speak Because Jesus Is Coming

In 4:1, Paul mentions Christ's "appearing" when he "will judge the living and the dead." He is, of course, referring to Jesus' second coming. The Bible teaches that a day is coming when the trumpet of the archangel will sound, the eastern sky will split, and Jesus will come riding back to earth on the clouds, followed by his angel armies. History will end, and all humanity will be judged—some to enjoy God's presence forever and others to eternal torment (Matt. 24:27–51; 25:31–46).

The Bible describes Christ's return in two ways. First, it will be *unexpected*. First Thessalonians 5:1–2 says he will come like a thief in the night. No thief ever gave his victims a courtesy call as advance warning, and we will have no advance notice of Christ's return.

Second, Christ's return will be *soon*. In Revelation 22, the last chapter of the Bible, Jesus says three times, "I am coming soon" (Rev. 22:7, 12, 20). All the prophecies to be fulfilled before his return have already taken place. There is nothing to prevent Jesus from crashing back through the clouds before you finish reading this sentence.

So if Jesus' return will be unexpected and soon, we must share the gospel with a sense of urgency. Who in your life still needs to hear about Christ? If you truly believe in heaven and hell, that person's eternal destiny hangs in the balance. Do not delay. I once heard someone say, "If Satan cannot convince us there is no heaven or hell, then he will convince us there is no *hurry*."

Paul says it differently. In verse two, "be prepared" was a Greek military word meaning "be on duty." The Message translates it: "Keep on your watch." As God's people, we're called to be vigilant in looking for opportunities to speak his message. We are to speak "in season"—when it's convenient. We are to speak "out of season"—when it's not convenient (2 Tim. 4:2).

In other words, we must *take* opportunities and *make* opportunities. John Stott writes, "We are given here not a biblical warrant for rudeness, but a biblical appeal against laziness."[2] If Jesus could return at any moment, then we must not grow lax in our responsibility as gospel messengers.

In speaking with others, however, we must be careful not to use a one-size-fits-all approach to evangelism and instead address each individual personally, tailoring our conversation to their unique needs:

- "Correct" and "rebuke" describe a *behavioral* approach. Some people are caught in sin and need to be confronted. They need you to speak to their *conscience*.
- "Encourage" describes an *emotional* approach. Some people are wounded by life and need to be strengthened. They need you to speak to their *heart*.
- "Careful instruction" describes an *intellectual* approach. Some people are troubled by doubts and need explanation. They need you to speak to their *mind*.

Paul adds that these spiritual conversations must be conducted "with great patience." When we care deeply about someone's spiritual destiny, we can get frustrated when they don't immediately embrace Christ as Lord. But conversion is a journey. Don't grow discouraged when someone doesn't instantly run all the way to the cross. Trust that each conversation can be a step in the right direction. Be patient. But this patience is not the same as passivity. Paul stresses that we must be proactive in our proclamation of Christ. I'm thinking of two quotes:

- I have a friend who keeps this sign on his office door: "Perhaps Today."
- I once saw a bumper sticker that said, "Jesus is coming. Look busy."

That's good advice. Jesus could in fact come back today, so we ought to be busy in the work of evangelism. We must speak God's message because Jesus is coming soon to judge the living and the dead. In his autobiography, *Just As I Am*, Billy Graham told of a golf outing with President John F. Kennedy, a Catholic. Kennedy asked Mr. Graham if he believed in the second coming of Jesus Christ. When Billy said he most certainly did, Kennedy asked, "Well, does my church believe it?" Mr. Graham said it was in the Catholic Church's creeds, to which President Kennedy replied, "They don't preach it. They don't tell us much about it. I'd like to know what you think."

After Billy explained what the Bible said about Christ's return, Kennedy replied, "Very interesting. We'll have to talk more about that someday." Here is Billy's conclusion to the story:

> The last time I was with Kennedy was at the 1963 National Prayer Breakfast. I had the flu. After we both gave our talks, we walked out of the hotel to his car together. At the curb, he turned to me. "Billy, could you ride back to the White House with me? I'd like to talk with you for a minute."
>
> "Mr. President, I've got a fever," I protested. "I don't want to give you this thing. Couldn't we wait and talk some other time?" It was a cold, snowy day, and I was freezing as I stood there without my overcoat. "Of course," he said graciously.[3]

Then came November 22, 1963, and Billy Graham never saw President Kennedy alive again. Reflecting back, he writes, "His hesitation at the car door, and his request, haunt me still. What was on his mind? Should I have gone with him? It was an irrecoverable moment."[4]

The truth is, we just don't know when our unsaved friends will stand before the judgment seat of Christ. That's why Paul writes elsewhere, "Be wise in the way you act toward outsiders; *make the most of every opportunity*" (Col. 4:5). When you see a conversational opening to speak about spiritual matters, take it. You don't know if you'll get another chance. It may be an irrecoverable moment.

Jesus is coming, and eternity hangs in the balance. Preach the Word.

Speak Because Satan Is Deceiving

A second reason Timothy is to speak God's message: he lives in a culture where truth is up for grabs. Paul says the people "turn their ears away from the truth and turn aside to myths" (4:4). The false teachers are saying whatever people want to hear. They are practicing "buffet-line spirituality"—picking the truths they like and leaving the ones they don't.

Ultimately, such spirituality is harmful for those who hear it. When Paul says that "people will not put up with sound doctrine," the Greek word for "sound" literally means *healthy* (4:3). The Message translates it this way: "People will have no stomach for solid teaching, but will fill up on spiritual junk food." A diet of false teaching—no matter how pleasant it may be to hear—will leave people spiritually anemic.

We too live in a world where truth is up for grabs. Everyone's beliefs are equally valid, our culture says. Your truth can conform to your taste—buffet-line spirituality.

So how are we to respond to such a culture? In 4:5, Paul gives four instructions:

1. *Keep your head on straight.* Don't be deceived by false teachers. The trouble with false teachers is that they smuggle 5 percent falsehood inside a package of 95 percent truth, so listen carefully. Some of these teachers enjoy great popularity—with bestselling books, big churches, and a large digital following. If we don't keep our wits about us, we can find ourselves falling for what "itching ears want to hear" (4:3).

2. *Expect hardship.* When we dare to speak the truth of Christ, we will not always be welcomed with open arms. When the apostles preached, they got one of two responses—either a revival or a riot. We too should expect some hits when we speak God's message, but don't give up. We may cause a riot or two, but somewhere we might start a revival.

3. *Share the gospel as good news.* This is what Paul means by "the work of an evangelist." An "evangelist" in ancient times was a messenger who came with an announcement of good news—victory in battle, an imperial holiday, or the birth of a child. No one dreaded the words of an evangelist. They welcomed him with excitement and anticipation. His words were filled with joy.

> **Every human heart hungers for God.**

Too often we act as if people will never want to hear what we have to say. Remember this: every human heart hungers for God. The false teachers may serve spiritual Twinkies and cotton candy, but a diet of junk food never satisfies anyone forever. We have the Bread of Life!

We get to share a truth that is both satisfying and life-giving. Don't treat the gospel like it's bad news.

4. *Don't give up.* Or as Paul puts it, "discharge all the duties of your ministry." Why? Because while some will not welcome us with excitement and anticipation, some will. That's why we must keep preaching the Word. Some people will realize that the emptiness in their soul is God-shaped. If we're not there to serve them "sound [healthy] doctrine," who will? We are God's plan for sharing the good news. There is no Plan B.

Satan is deceiving people, and only the truth can set them free. Preach the Word.

Speak Because Paul Is Leaving

The final reason Timothy must speak God's message is simple but poignant: Paul won't be around to do it himself anymore. As Paul writes from the Mamertine Prison in Rome, he knows his time is short. In a few weeks, the executioner's sword will fall. Paul uses several metaphors to describe his impending death.

- "Poured out like a drink offering" is a *sacrificial* metaphor, taken from Numbers 15:5–10. (See also Phil. 2:17.) Paul says his life was an act of worship, given in gratitude to God.
- Paul also uses a *nautical* metaphor. "Departure" pictures a boat losing its moorings. Of Paul's many ocean voyages, he is ready now for his last, which will carry him safely to heaven's shore.
- "Fought the good fight" is a *military* metaphor. At the end of the day of battle, he stands exhausted—his sword arm heavy, his strength spent. Others must carry on the fight in days ahead.
- Paul then employs an *athletic* metaphor. He often compared the Christian life to a race (1 Cor. 9:24–27; Gal. 5:7; Phil. 3:14). Now he says he has "finished the race" and will receive the victor's crown.

The athletic imagery reminds me of my high school track experience. I ran the third leg of the 4x800 meter relay, and I vividly remember leaning forward at the starting line, palms sweating, heart beating out of my chest. I searched the pack of second leg runners as they rounded the last curve, locked eyes with my teammate, and stuck out my hand. He slapped the baton into my palm, and I took off, running for all I was worth. Why did I run so hard? Yes, I wanted to achieve a personal best time, up my game. But I also knew my teammates who had run before me were counting on me.

Here Paul is saying to Timothy, *I have finished my leg of the race, and now I'm passing the baton to you, Timothy. I'm counting on you to continue my work, so run hard and hold on tight.* Paul is leaving, so now Timothy must take over preaching the Word. As Joshua followed Moses, as Elisha followed Elijah, so Timothy must follow Paul.

Who passed the baton to you? Someone spoke God's message to you—maybe a friend, your parents, a minister, a grandparent, or a coworker. Someone told them about Jesus, and then they told you. Will that chain remain unbroken? Will you, in turn, tell someone else about Jesus, or will the message stop with you? The baton has been passed, and now you must continue the legacy of someone else's ministry.

Who Will Fill His Shoes?

When I was a Bible college student, I accepted a part-time youth ministry position at a church in town. The preacher, Bob Ely, quickly became a trusted mentor. Bob was the definition of high energy, a dirt bike racer and a biplane pilot. He never walked; he just sort of bounced from one place to another, with a mischievous sparkle in his eye and a smile underneath his mustache.

One of my first memories of Bob was when I'd only been working at the church for a week, and Valentine's Day was that Friday. I couldn't afford to take my fiancée, Katie, to a nice restaurant, so I asked Bob if I could use the church office that night. He said yes, so I set up a card table with a red tablecloth and a candle. I could afford a half gallon of ice cream, so I scooped out two Styrofoam plates of ice cream, sculpted them into heart shapes, lined them with Red Hots, and put them in the freezer. (Sappy? Yes, but cheap.)

That evening, I took Katie out to the darkened church and surprised her. As we sat there eating our ice cream by candlelight, guess who appeared at the office door with a guitar in hand? Bob never said a word. He just smiled, serenaded us with two love songs, and then disappeared into the night. It was hard not to like Bob.

He was a solid preacher. I remember one sermon he preached from Deuteronomy 31. He placed a pair of sandals by the pulpit and talked about Joshua filling Moses's sandals, succeeding him as leader. Then Bob placed a pair of black dress shoes by the sandals and talked about John Martin, a long-time faithful elder who had recently passed away. He asked, "Who will fill John Martin's shoes?"

It was a good sermon, but Bob did his best preaching one-on-one. He'd grab me and say, "Come on, Proctor. Let's go talk to some people about Jesus." We'd hop in his red Mazda pickup, go to the Dairy Queen not far from the church, and talk to the ladies behind the counter about Jesus. We went to living rooms, hospital rooms, the bleachers at kids' ball games and talked with people about Jesus.

Bob kept a pair of muddy work boots in the back of his truck. He'd drive up Highway 43 to Chism's farm, throw on his boots, and work out in the field alongside Jay Chism, talking about Jesus. Jay and Mindy Chism still attend that church. Bob preached his best sermons in farm fields, on front porch swings, and over restaurant counters, and I was there watching, listening, and learning.

I graduated from Bible college and became the preacher of a little church in Carbondale, Illinois. I'd only been there nine months when I got a phone call telling me Bob's biplane had crashed. He was killed instantly.

Katie and I drove back to Missouri for his funeral. That little church of 150 where I'd been the youth minister was crowded with over 300 people—lives that Bob had touched. As I sat in the pew listening to the funeral message, I couldn't help but imagine a pair of muddy work boots sitting there by the pulpit.

Who would take Bob's place? Who would fill his shoes?

I drove back to my ministry in Illinois. I helped a farm family put up hay, went to kids' ball games, sat in living rooms and hospital rooms and on front porch swings. I visited the Dairy Queen three blocks from our church. And everywhere I went, I tried to talk about Jesus. I can't help but think: somehow Bob's ministry lived on in me.

Whose ministry lives on in you? Someone passed you the baton. Don't drop it. Tell someone else about Jesus. Speak God's message. Take the apostle Paul's last words as a personal charge to you.

Preach the Word.

Discussion Questions

1. In your last moments on earth, what might you be thinking about?
2. What might change if you saw yourself as a missionary to those people in your sphere of influence?
3. Each verb in 2 Timothy 4:2 describes a different approach to speaking with people. Think of a person you want to reach. What approach might be most effective for them?
4. When have you felt discouraged in your efforts to witness to someone?
5. Who passed you the baton and told you about Jesus?

TAKE ACTION Ask God to open conversational doors and give you the courage to pass the baton to someone else.

11

Cultivate Real Community

2 Timothy 4:9–15, 19–22

"Call it a clan, call it a tribe, call it a network, call it a family. Whatever you call it, whoever you are, you need one."

— JANE HOWARD

Several years ago, two of my nephews accompanied their mom on a visit to a friend's house. Ben was eight, Brian was six. Their mother's friend was a very neat lady—a place for everything and everything in its place. She had defeated clutter and driven it from her home. Though childless, she did have a few toys and handed Ben and Brian a bucket of Legos: "Here, boys, you can play with these."

What's the first thing they did with that bucket? Like all red-blooded American boys, they dumped it out. Their mother's uptight friend immediately went into full obsessive cleaning mode. She dropped to her knees and started scooping the Lego pieces back into the bucket with these words: "No, no, no, boys. What I meant was, you can play with these . . . one at a time."

What?

You might be able to play with dolls or Hot Wheels one at a time, but *you can't play with Legos one at time!* A Lego piece is created to be part of a group, something bigger than itself. A solitary Lego can never fulfill its destiny. Legos were made to be connected.

Lego Theology

You don't have to read far into your Bible to discover that human beings were created to be combined with other human beings. In Genesis 1, God makes the world and declares, "It is good." But after creating man, God says, "It is *not* good." Why? Because the man is alone. There's only one of him, and humans aren't meant to do life one at a time. So God decides to split the Adam. (I know, bad joke.) He makes Eve from Adam's rib to be his life partner, and only then can God say, "It is very good." Call it Lego theology: human beings were made to be connected. We were created for community.

This is because we are created in God's image (Gen. 1:27). God is Trinity—completely one, yet in three persons. From eternity past, the Father, Son, and Spirit have lived together in perfect community. Since before the beginning of time, the Father, Son, and Spirit have enjoyed each other, served each other, valued each other, understood each other, and loved each other. At the center of the universe lives a divine community—three persons who are inseparably and wonderfully *connected*.

As humans created in God's image, we too are made for relationship. A solitary human being can never fulfill their destiny. You will never finish well on your own—literally. A landmark Harvard study of 7,000 people found that the most isolated people were three times more likely to die than those with strong relationships.[1] Reporting on the study, one psychologist wrote that "people who had bad health habits (such as smoking, poor eating habits, or alcohol use) but strong social ties lived *significantly longer* than people who had great health habits but were isolated. In other words, it is better to eat Twinkies with good friends than to eat broccoli alone."[2]

What is true physically is also true spiritually: we need community. That's why God invented the church. The Christian life is meant to be lived together. Too many in our culture say they're committed to Jesus but not the church. Disillusioned with imperfect churches, they take a "just me and Jesus" approach.

But not even Jesus did that. He gathered a very imperfect community of twelve to share life with. Jesus didn't begin the Lord's

Prayer, "*My* Father who art in heaven." He taught us to pray "*Our* Father." While the gospel is certainly personal, it is never individual. If you belong to Jesus, you also belong to everyone else who belongs to Jesus. Imperfect as it is, the church is part of the package.

> **Imperfect as it is, the church is part of the package.**

Don't Skip the Final Paragraphs

The apostle Paul knew this deep in his bones. Too often, we picture Paul as the great solo missionary, a lone evangelist moving from one church plant to the next. That may be because we instinctively skip the closing sections of Paul's letters labeled "Personal Remarks" or "Final Greetings." No real substance there, right?

Not true. These final paragraphs teach us something immensely important: Paul never did life alone. Read Romans 16, 1 Corinthians 16, or Colossians 4, and you'll find dozens of names—people Paul constantly leaned on for encouragement, partnership, and wisdom. Paul was wary of what someone once called "the peril of the solitary life."[3] So he gathered around him a "band of brothers," a little community of faith to uphold him. He stayed connected.

Yet here in prison in 2 Timothy 4, Paul feels almost completely isolated, cut off from those close to him:

- Demas deserted him because "he loved this world" (4:10). Was it fleshly temptation or fear for his own life that pulled Demas from Paul's side? This close associate's abandonment—elsewhere Paul calls him a "fellow worker"—must have pained the apostle deeply (Philem. 24).
- Crescens and Titus traveled to Galatia and Dalmatia, respectively (4:10). Since Paul doesn't criticize his coworkers for not being there, they were presumably on legitimate kingdom business, but they were absent nonetheless.
- Tychicus was on his way to Ephesus with the letter of 2 Timothy in hand (4:12).

- After Paul's arrest, Erastus and Trophimus had apparently been traveling with Paul to Rome (4:20). But when they arrived in Corinth, Erastus left the apostle to stay in his hometown (Rom. 16:23). Trophimus made it as far as Miletus before succumbing to illness.
- Only Luke, the faithful doctor, is still at Paul's side (4:11). Can you picture these two old men sitting together in the Roman prison cell? Balding but for a few wisps of gray hair, ragged clothes, shivering when temperatures drop at night?

Paul is lonely, so as he closes the letter, he urges Timothy to get Mark and visit him in Rome. Winter is coming when the seas are closed to traffic. If Timothy waits until spring, he may end up visiting Paul's grave instead of his prison cell. So he says, "Do your best to get here before winter" (4:21).

He asks Timothy to stop in Troas—which may be where Paul was arrested—to gather a few things he left there. (While there, Timothy must be on guard against Alexander. The Greek form of the verb "did me a great deal of harm" literally means "to inform against" [4:14]. Was Alexander the informer responsible for Paul's arrest?) Paul wants his books, especially his Bible, for the sake of his mind. He wants his cloak for the sake of his body. But most of all, he wants the companionship of Timothy and Mark for the sake of his soul.

Though Nelson Mandela was imprisoned for twenty-seven years, he emerged to lead South Africa out of apartheid. His relationships with his fellow political prisoners sustained him through years of intense suffering. In his autobiography, he wrote:

> It would be very hard if not impossible for one man alone to resist. But the authorities' greatest mistake was to keep us together, for together our determination was reinforced. We supported each other and gained strength from each other. Whatever we learned, we shared, and by sharing we multiplied whatever courage we had individually. The stronger ones raised up the weaker ones, and both became stronger in the process.[4]

Paul knows that in community, his courage will be multiplied, so he pleads with Timothy to come quickly. But the wise apostle is surely seeking to multiply Timothy's courage as well. He wants to model for "timid Timothy" the strength found in real Christian fellowship.

Fellowship in Scripture (the Greek word *koinonia*) is more than church potluck dinners. When I was growing up, the church congregation would gather in the fellowship hall, eat casserole, and talk about the weather, the football game, and our trucks' gas mileage. We called it fellowship. This is Christian *socializing*, which can be a great joy.

But the difference between Christian socializing and Christian fellowship is the difference between eating a donut and eating a square meal—one is fun, but the other is necessary for health. True Christian *koinonia* happens when we get past surface conversation, crack the door on our hearts, and share our spiritual life together.

When fellowship happens, we talk about what we don't understand about the Bible, what God is teaching us as we read, where we're struggling in our lives, who we're serving, who's frustrating us, what decisions we face, and the blessings we're experiencing. We encourage, admonish, comfort, challenge, serve, rejoice with, mourn with, submit to, forgive, share with, bear with, care for, and pray for one another. That's *koinonia*, and when this is cultivated, our courage to persevere through tough times is multiplied. By mentioning the names in this section, Paul suggests at least three things Timothy can find in real Christian community: a *warm welcome*, a *second chance*, and a *helping hand*.

Community Includes a Warm Welcome

As you reflect on the names in 2 Timothy 4, their diversity is striking. This is not a homogenous group of people. You find differences in the following:

- *Occupation:* Luke is a doctor (Col. 4:14). Erastus is a politician (Rom. 16:13). Priscilla and Aquila are tentmakers (Acts 18:2–3).

- *Age:* Timothy and Mark are younger thirtysomethings. Paul and Luke are likely in their sixties.
- *Gender:* Some Jewish rabbis viewed women as second-class citizens, daily praying, "Thank you, God, for not making me a Gentile, a slave, or a woman."[5] Paul, however, speaks of Priscilla and Claudia as valued fellow believers.
- *Race:* Paul and Mark are Jewish. Titus and Luke are Greeks. Timothy is half-Jewish, half-Greek. Pudens and Linus are Roman.

Despite these differences, they are family. Paul's favorite term for Christ-followers is "brothers"—over "saints," "Christians," or "believers." More than sixty times he refers to fellow believers as "brothers" in his letters, including here in our text (4:21). In a world where prejudices run high, each person in this diverse list has been given a warm welcome into the family of God. They have taken to heart Paul's words in Romans 15:7, "Accept one another, then, just as Christ accepted you."

When I served as a preacher in Carbondale, Illinois, I became friends with a young man in our congregation named Aminu Timberlake. Aminu played basketball for Southern Illinois University, and through his roommate's witness, he became a Christian and joined our church. He came to me with questions about the Bible. We talked often and enjoyed joking around together. I performed at his wedding. So when I was preparing to leave that ministry, Aminu made sure to stop by to say his goodbyes. He gave me a big bear hug with these words: "You and me, we've got to stay in touch because you and me—we're like family."

To anyone eavesdropping on that moment, those would've been strange words. Aminu is black; I'm white. Aminu is six-foot-nine; I'm five-foot-nine. Aminu grew up in a tough neighborhood on Chicago's south side; I grew up in small-town Iowa. Aminu was from a family of lifelong Democrats; my dad's initials (honest truth) are GOP. Aminu was big man on campus, a starter for a Division I basketball program.

I was the unknown preacher of a little church on the west side of town. You probably couldn't have found two guys more different.

Family? Absolutely. As Bob Russell says, "A man doesn't have to be my twin to be my brother." In the community of Christ, despite our differences, we welcome each other as he welcomed us. Paul wants Timothy to stay connected because, though the world may reject him, he will always find a warm welcome in the family of God.

Community Includes a Second Chance

When you're different from others, the offer of a warm welcome is a kindness; but when you're disappointing to others, the offer of a second chance is nothing short of a marvel. That's because the law of this world is justice, not grace. You've heard it said when one person has betrayed another: "They'll get what's coming to them. What goes around comes around." The default human setting is not forgiveness; it's revenge. Second chances aren't our first instinct.

But things are different in the community of faith. Take Mark, for example. He accompanied Paul and his cousin Barnabas on the apostle's first missionary journey but deserted them before the journey was over (Acts 13:13). Was he homesick, afraid of bandits, or intimidated by the stiff climb over the Taurus mountains? We don't know. But we do know that when Barnabas suggested taking Mark along on their second missionary journey, Paul's disappointment ran so deep that he split from Barnabas rather than travel again with Mark (Acts 15:38–39). Paul wasn't ready to give him a second chance.

Ever felt like that? I once heard about a guy who dialed a friend's phone number and got this message: "I am not available right now, but thank you for caring enough to call. I am making some changes in my life. Please leave a message after the beep. If I do not return your call, you are one of the changes."

The fact is, sometimes we wish we could just delete difficult people from our lives. The Bible is honest about the challenges of living in community. The New Testament does not paint a picture of the church as people who live together in perpetual harmony. Community gets messy, and that's why there are scriptural admonitions like:

- Be patient with one another (implied: "because people will annoy you").
- Bear with one another (implied: "because people will aggravate you").
- Forgive one another (implied: "because people will hurt you").

When someone disappoints us, we are tempted to wash our hands of them. But Dietrich Bonhoeffer wrote that true community *begins* with disappointment.[6] Real *koinonia* begins when we painfully realize that someone isn't perfect—and we choose to love them anyway. We can't love people for who we wish they were. We can only love them for who they are.

So we forgive and go on. Forgiveness doesn't mean that we fail to deal with the conflict. I heard someone say there is a difference between peace*making* and peace*faking*—one works through difficulties while the other ignores them. Forgiving is not just forgetting. Instead, forgiveness involves releasing your anger and seeking to reconnect in appropriate ways. We refuse to turn our back on the one who hurt us. As a mentor once told me, "Godly leaders have no disposable relationships."

Eventually, Paul realized this, forgave Mark, and offered him a second chance. Now he wants to see Mark before he dies and calls him "helpful to me in my ministry" (4:11). That's the beauty of Christian community: *our failures are not fatal.* We receive grace, and Paul wants Timothy to stay connected because only in the church will he find a second chance.

Community Includes a Helping Hand

Finally, Paul knows firsthand that Timothy will find in Christian fellowship a helping hand when he needs it. He mentions Priscilla and Aquila who at some point, he says in Romans 16:4, "risked their lives for me." The Greek could literally be translated "stuck their necks out for me"—a figure of speech not to be taken lightly in an age when the executioner's axe was not a metaphor. This courageous couple had placed themselves in great peril to help their friend Paul.

Paul also references Onesiphorus, whose name means "profitable" and who was mentioned earlier in the letter (1:16–18; 4:19). There he said Onesiphorus came to Rome from Ephesus and searched hard for the aged prisoner, likely taking his life in his hands to do so.

Paul says that Onesiphorus "often refreshed" him and, earlier in Ephesus, had "helped" him in many ways (1:16, 18). This is at the core of true Christian community. We help each other. Whether it's financial assistance, a listening ear, lawn mowing, babysitting, a car to borrow, advice on parenting, a shoulder to cry on, or a place to stay, we do what we can to meet each other's needs. One of the most amazing statements made of the early church is that, because of the many helping hands, "there were no needy persons among them" (Acts 4:34).

> **This is at the core of Christian community. We help each other.**

Pastor Stu Weber paints a picture of this level of helping community with a story from his days in Army Ranger training:

> We'd been running every day, but this was something else. This was the physical training stage of US Army Ranger School, and we expected exertion, even exhaustion. But this was no morning PT rah-rah run in T-shirts. We ran in full field uniform. Loaded packs. Helmets. Boots. Rifles. As usual, the word was, "You go out together, you stick together, and you come in together. If you don't come in together, don't bother to come in!"
>
> Somewhere along the way, I noticed one of the guys was out of sync: a big, rawboned redhead named Sanderson. His legs were pumping, but he was out of step with the rest of us. Then his head began to loll from side to side. This guy was struggling—close to losing it.
>
> Without missing a step, the Ranger on Sanderson's right reached over and took the distressed man's rifle. Now one of the Rangers was packing two weapons—his own and Sanderson's. The big redhead did better for a time. But then while the platoon kept moving, his jaw became slack, his eyes glazed, and soon he began to sway again. This time, the ranger on his left reached over,

removed Sanderson's helmet, tucked it under his own arm, and continued to run. All systems go. Our boots thudded along the dirt trail in heavy unison. Tromp-tromp-tromp-tromp!

Sanderson was hurting, really hurting. He was buckling, going down. But no, two soldiers behind him lifted the pack off his back, each taking a shoulder strap in his free hand. Sanderson gathered his remaining strength, squared his shoulders, and the platoon continued to run—all the way to the finish line. We left together. We returned together. And all of us were the stronger for it.

Together is better.[7]

Don't skip the final paragraphs of this letter to Timothy. In this list of names, Paul's message to Timothy is powerful: *beware the peril of the solitary life*. Don't try to go it alone. If you want to cross the finish line of faith, stay connected. Together with other believers, you will find a warm welcome. Together with other believers, you will find a second chance. Together with other believers, you will find a helping hand.

Together is better.

Discussion Questions

1. Do you know people who say they are Christians but have nothing to do with the church? How does this square with what we see in the New Testament?
2. What are some of the "perils of the solitary life"?
3. Who is in your "band of brothers" you do life with?
4. When have you had *koinonia*? What can you do to pursue this kind of community now?
5. Bonhoeffer said that true community *begins* with disappointment. What does it take to forgive and offer a second chance?

TAKE ACTION Thank God for Christian community. Ask him for patience when people disappoint you. Thank him for others' patience with you.

12

Stay Close to Jesus

2 Timothy 4:16–18

*"Peace is not the absence of affliction,
but the presence of God."*

— ANONYMOUS

A mother washing dishes after dinner asked her little boy to go out on the back porch to get the broom. Out of the corner of her eye, she watched her five-year-old go to the back door, open it, and look out for a few moments before returning to sit at the kitchen table. Sensing what was wrong, she sat down at the table. "You're scared of the dark, aren't you?" she asked her son. He nodded his head.

His mother smiled reassuringly, "You don't have to be afraid, honey. Remember: Jesus is always with you. That means he's right out there on that back porch too, so you don't have to be afraid. Okay?"

"Okay, Mama," he said. His mother went back to her dishes and watched again as her son went to the back door. He cracked it open, poked his head out, but still didn't step out. "Jesus, I know you're right out here on this back porch with me," she heard him say. "So do you mind handing me that broom over there?"

When you face difficult times, the presence of Christ makes all the difference.

In our study of 2 Timothy, we've looked at several ways to develop finish-line

> **In difficult times, the presence of Christ makes all the difference.**

faith. But in this race called the Christian life, the most important thing is this: *stay close to Jesus.* When the writer of Hebrews wrote, "Let us run with perseverance the race marked out for us," he followed it immediately with, "fixing our eyes on Jesus" (Heb. 12:1–2). That's because:

- When we are afraid, Jesus gives us courage;
- When we are weary, Jesus gives us strength;
- When we are confused, Jesus gives us guidance;
- When we are grieving, Jesus gives us comfort; and
- When we are guilty, Jesus gives us grace.

Second Timothy 2:1 is a pivotal verse in this letter. Paul tells Timothy, "You then, my son, be strong in the grace that is in Christ Jesus." Paul is wise. Telling Timothy to be strong in his own strength would have been "futile, even absurd," John Stott writes. "He might as well have told a snail to be quick or a horse to fly as command a man as timid as Timothy to be strong."[1]

But Paul isn't telling Timothy to be strong in himself. Timothy is to find his strength *in Christ.* In fact, "be strong" is a passive verb—literally, "be strengthened." This is not something Timothy does; rather it's something done to Timothy. In John 15:5, Jesus said, "I am the vine; you are the branches. If you remain in me and I in you, you will bear much fruit; apart from me you can do nothing." Timothy's job is simply to remain in Jesus; Jesus' job is to give him the strength to cross the finish line.

A Testimony of Christ's Faithful Presence

Paul knows this better than anyone. For more than thirty years, he has leaned on Jesus. He is painfully aware of his own limitations; he knows he cannot do it on his own. So the apostle counts on the great promise the Lord made to him: "My grace is sufficient for you, for my power is made perfect in weakness" (2 Cor. 12:9).

Nowhere do we see this more clearly than in 2 Timothy 4:16–18. These are the last of Paul's last words, the final message of his last recorded letter. In the closing camera shot before the end credits roll, we see Paul in his Roman prison cell, reflecting on Christ's faithful presence.

Jesus had promised that he would never leave or forsake his own, that he would be with them "always, to the very end of the age" (Matt. 28:20). Paul is testifying that Jesus has kept his promise.

Paul says in 4:16–17, "At my first defense, no one came to my support, but everyone deserted me . . . . But the Lord stood at my side and gave me strength." In a Roman trial, an initial hearing was held to determine if a full-blown trial was needed, and Paul says none of his friends stepped forward at this hearing to act as his advocates or witnesses. Yet he sensed Christ beside him, strengthening him (Phil. 4:13).

In fact, Jesus gave Paul the boldness to seize this moment to proclaim the gospel so that "all the Gentiles might hear it." John Stott vividly paints the picture: "In one of the highest tribunals of the empire, before his judges and perhaps before the emperor himself, no doubt with a large crowd of the general public present, Paul 'preached the word.'"[2] In 4:2, Paul has just charged Timothy to preach the Word "in season and out of season," and the old preacher is not telling Timothy to do anything he hasn't done himself. Instead of pleading his own case at his hearing, Paul seized the moment to plead the case of Christ. That's finishing strong!

Paul's testimony goes on: "And I was delivered from the lion's mouth" (4:17). Paul was spared immediate death, he says, because Christ delivered him just as he had delivered Daniel in the Old Testament. Back then, Daniel appeared powerless but was never out of the safekeeping of his God. As William Augustus once wrote, "Daniel was not in the lion's den. The lions were in Daniel's den."[3] So too the apostle is confident that Jesus, not the emperor, is in complete control of his situation.

This is why he can write, "The Lord will rescue me from every evil attack and will bring me safely to his heavenly kingdom" (4:18). That's Romans 8:28 confidence! You remember the verse he boldly wrote to the church in Rome: "We know that in all things God works for the good of those who love him, who have been called according to his purpose." He wrote those words years ago from the city of Corinth with relative ease. It's much easier to write Romans 8:28 when you're not in a Roman prison. Does he still believe those words now?

The answer is a resounding yes! He still trusts God. Paul is finishing well—still preaching, still praying, still encouraging, still trusting—for one simple reason: he is close to Jesus, and he knows Jesus is close to him.

How can we cultivate the awareness of Christ's presence with us? How can we experience the closeness with Jesus that Paul felt? This text hints at four ways: through *Scripture meditation, continuous communion, faithful suffering,* and *joyful singing.*

Stay Close Through Scripture Meditation

Many scholars have noted echoes of Psalm 22 throughout this text. Jesus quoted Psalm 22 on the cross, and as Paul faces his own imminent execution, he appears to be meditating on the same passage.

Psalm 22	2 Timothy 4
"Why have you forsaken me?"	"All men forsook me" (KJV).
"There is no one to help."	"No one came to my support."
"Rescue me from the mouth of the lions."	"I was delivered from the lion's mouth."
"All the ends of the earth will turn to the LORD."	"All the Gentiles might hear it."
"Deliver me from the sword . . . from the power of the dogs . . . from the horns of the wild oxen."	"The Lord will rescue me from every evil attack."

One of the ways Paul stays close to Jesus is by meditating on his Word. When we face the greatest trials of our lives, we will encounter the presence of Christ in the pages of his Word.

A preacher I heard once recounted a story from the well-known missionary Elisabeth Elliot. She told the story of a toddler many years ago who was very ill, and her parents had taught her to recite the first line of Psalm 23 on her fingers. Starting with her pinkie, she would grab a finger as she said each word: "The LORD is my shepherd." As she said the word "shepherd," she would clasp her thumb in recognition of God's care for her. When her pain was great, she found comfort in reciting this verse.

One morning, after a long and hard fight against her disease, her parents found that their little girl had passed away in the night. They found her with one hand clasped around the other thumb. She died knowing she was in the care of the Great Shepherd, and now he would lead her to green pastures and quiet waters. Now she would dwell in the house of the Lord forever. In that Scripture, Christ was with her in her hour of need.

If you want to stay close to Jesus, meditate on his Word.

Stay Close Through Continuous Communion

In 4:22, Paul prays for Timothy, "The Lord be with your spirit." He wants Timothy to have a constant sense of Christ's presence with him. Paul certainly kept a continuous communion with Christ, an ongoing awareness of his presence, a sense of uninterrupted conversation with Christ as he went about his daily affairs. Sometimes this is called "the practice of the presence of God."

A missionary named Frank Laubach wrote of his attempt to "practice the presence":

> Jesus walked along the road day after day "God-intoxicated" and radiant with the endless communion of His soul with God . . . .
> Can we have that contact with God all the time? . . . Can I bring the Lord back in my mindflow every few seconds so that God

shall always be in my mind? I choose to make the rest of my life an experiment in answering this question.[4]

Consider some of these ways Frank sought to stay close to Jesus:

- Set an extra chair at the table to remind you that Christ is the unseen guest at every meal.
- When reading books, articles, or emails, read them *to Jesus*. Frank Laubach wrote, "Have you ever opened a letter and read it with Jesus, realizing that he smiles with us at the fun, rejoices with us in the successes, and weeps with us in the tragedies? If not, you have missed one of life's sweetest experiences."[5]
- When going about your business or chewing on a problem at work, instead of talking to yourself, talk to Christ. Laubach wrote, "Many of us who have tried this have found that we think so much better that we never want to try to think without Him again!"[6]
- Keep a picture of Jesus where you will see it as you go to sleep. Let your eyes and thoughts begin there again first thing in the morning to remind you of his ongoing companionship.

"This way of life," one author observes, "opened him wide to spiritual reality and power that was all around him all the time, like a radio antenna suddenly tuned in to the right frequency."[7]

Surely this is what Paul is praying for Timothy when he says, "The Lord be with your spirit" (4:22). He wants Timothy to find finish-line strength through practicing the presence of Christ.

If you want to stay close to Jesus, commune constantly with him.

Stay Close Through Faithful Suffering

When asking how Paul could experience such closeness to Christ, don't overlook the apostle's circumstances. He is in prison, awaiting execution. The fact is that Paul spent roughly one-quarter of his missionary career in prisons. We may not realize what that meant or looked like. Professor John McRay describes it:

Roman imprisonment was preceded by being stripped naked and then flogged—a humiliating, painful, and bloody ordeal. The bleeding wounds went untreated as prisoners sat in painful leg or wrist chains. Mutilated, bloodstained clothing was not replaced, even in the cold of winter. Most cells were dark, especially the inner cells of a prison, like the one Paul and Silas inhabited in Philippi. Unbearable cold, lack of water, cramped quarters, and sickening stench from few toilets made sleeping difficult and waking hours miserable. Because of the miserable conditions, many prisoners begged for a speedy death. Others simply committed suicide.[8]

Yet in brutal settings like this, the apostle Paul wrote encouraging, even joyful, letters. How? Because there is something about suffering that brings us closer to Jesus. In Philippians 3:10, Paul writes, "I want to know Christ—yes, to know the power of his resurrection." Paul's consuming passion was to know Jesus—next to that, all other pursuits were just as worthless as throwaway garbage. This verse resonates with us; we think, *Yes, I want to know Jesus too. I too want to feel his resurrection power coursing through my life!* But Paul doesn't end the verse there. The last phrase of Philippians 3:10 reads, "I want . . . participation in his sufferings, becoming like him in his death." Read that carefully: Paul wants to know Christ so badly that when he discovers that suffering draws him closer to Jesus, he *wants* to experience suffering.

Don't take this to mean that Paul is a spiritual masochist who finds strange pleasure in pain. The apostle has discovered a secret: you never feel any closer to Jesus than when you're hanging on to him in the midst of suffering. So while Paul doesn't purposely seek out persecution, neither does he seek to avoid it at all costs. Paul knows he will experience an extraordinary fellowship with Jesus that is found only in the midst of great trial.

Think about this biblically:

- It is only in the fiery furnace that Shadrach, Meshach, and Abednego get to walk side by side with one "like a son of the gods" (Dan. 3:25).

- It is only as Stephen faces death as the first martyr that he sees a vision of Jesus standing at God's right hand (Acts 7:56).
- It is only when the apostle John is exiled to the island of Patmos that he gets to see a vision of the glorified Christ (Rev. 1:13).

These believers experienced a fellowship with Christ in suffering that they had never experienced before. Does this mean you ought to seek out suffering? That you somehow should arrange for trials to happen in your life? By no means. But it does mean that when you experience suffering, you can expect to know Jesus in a way you've never known him before.

> If you want to stay close to Jesus, don't avoid suffering.

If you want to stay close to Jesus, don't avoid suffering.

Stay Close Through Joyful Singing

Paul was a singer. Remember when he and Silas were beaten and imprisoned in Philippi? I think I would be moaning and complaining, but not Paul. Acts 16:25 says, "About midnight Paul and Silas were praying and singing hymns to God, and the other prisoners were listening to them." He was singing! Throughout his letters, scholars tell us that Paul often quoted pieces of ancient Christian hymns. His letters often include prayers called doxologies, which sometimes insert themselves right in the middle of the chapter. Apparently, Paul would get so caught up in the truth he was writing that before moving on to his next point, he would just break out into musical praise.

In other words, when you feel like giving up, sing.

When my wife, Katie, and I were students in Bible college, a group of students would go each Friday night to a local nursing home to visit the residents. That's where I met Raymond. My wife had known Raymond since she was a little girl. She could remember Raymond being wheeled into church every Sunday morning.

Raymond had multiple sclerosis and was probably in his forties when I met him. His mind was sharp, but he was a prisoner in his own body. He was confined to a bed day after day in the nursing home because he could not take care of himself.

Each Friday night when Raymond saw us coming, a crooked smile would spread across his face. Katie and I would stand on either side of his bed and grab one of his hands, and through labored speech, Raymond would request that we sing the same song with him every week. I had never heard the song before, but Katie and Raymond taught it to me. Every Friday, Raymond would smile and sing:

> I'm so happy, I'm so happy
> I'm so happy, happy, happy, happy, happy, happy, happy
> I'm so happy, I'm so happy
> 'Cause Jesus is a friend of mine.

No matter how hard I thought my week had been, I never walked out of that nursing home without a song on my lips.

Paul was just like Raymond. In the midst of physical pain, heart-break, loneliness, and loss, Paul could still sing because he sensed the companionship of Jesus. At the end of this letter of 2 Timothy, Paul knows Jesus is near and writes, "The Lord will rescue me from every evil attack and will bring me safely to his heavenly kingdom." Do you know what the next line in 2 Timothy 4:18 is?

It's a doxology: "To him be glory forever and ever. Amen." Paul goes out singing.

If you want to stay close to Jesus, keep singing.

One Last Story

E. Stanley Jones was a missionary to India who reached hundreds of thousands with the gospel. At age eighty-eight, after sixty-five years of ministry, he suffered a stroke that crippled him. In the last few months before he died, E. Stanley Jones managed to dictate through virtually paralyzed lips the manuscript of a remarkable book.

In one paragraph he says:

> There are scars on my faith, but underneath those scars, there are no doubts. [Christ] has me with the consent of all my being and

with the cooperation of all my life. The song I sing is a lit song. Not the temporary exuberance of youth that often fades when middle and old age sets in with their disillusionment and cynicism . . . . No, I'm eighty-eight, and I'm more excited today about being a Christian than I was at eighteen when I first put my feet upon the way.[9]

That's finish-line faith.

Remember the Big Jake Principle from Chapter 1: *It's not how you start the race that matters. It's how you finish.* When you feel tired and weary and worn, read through this book of 2 Timothy again. Let the Spirit-inspired words of Paul breathe new life into your soul. May you sense the presence of Jesus close at your side, and may you sing "a lit song."

And no matter what happens: don't quit.

Discussion Questions

1. When have you most strongly felt the presence of Jesus?
2. Have you ever heard of "practicing the presence of Christ"? What do you think of the idea of conscious communion with Jesus throughout the day?
3. When you hear that a way we fellowship with Christ is through suffering, do you wish it weren't true? Why do you think it is true?
4. How do you incorporate singing or worship music into your life apart from church?
5. When you finish your race, what would you like others to say about you? Are you living in such a way now to compel that?

TAKE ACTION Thank God for the book of 2 Timothy. Thank him for the promise that he will always be with us, and ask him to help you intentionally look for and pursue his constant presence.

Notes

1 | When You Feel Like Giving In

1. John Stott, *The Message of 2 Timothy* (Downers Grove, IL: IVP, 1973), 30.

2. Steve Farrar, *Finishing Strong* (Sisters, OR: Multnomah, 1995), 16.

3. Adapted from Stott, *The Message of 2 Timothy*, 26.

4. Quoted in "The China Missions Quote Project," *Vision for China*, accessed March 25, 2024, visionforchina.org/the-china-missions-quote-project.

2 | Remember Your Heritage

1. You may remember that David Livingstone was the nineteenth-century Scottish missionary, doctor, and explorer who helped open central Africa to missions.

2. J. K. Jones, *Reading with God in Mind* (Joplin, MO: Heartspring, 2003), 60–61.

3. Tim Hansel, *Holy Sweat* (Dallas, TX: W Publishing, 1989), 26.

3 | Rely on the Spirit

1. The *l* and *i* reference is from John Ortberg, *The Life You've Always Wanted* (Grand Rapids, MI: Zondervan, 1997), 107.

2. Cited in Jack Cottrell, *The Holy Spirit: A Biblical Study* (Joplin, MO: College Press, 2006), 8.

3. Leslie Flynn, *19 Gifts of the Spirit* (Wheaton, IL: Victor, 1994), 16.

4. William Barclay, *The Letters to Timothy, Titus and Philemon*, Daily Study Bible (Louisville, KY: Westminster John Knox, 1975), 144.

5. Andrée Seu Peterson, "The Power of Now," *WORLD Magazine*, October 29, 2005, accessed May 30, 2024, wng.org/articles/the-power-of-now-1617337604.

6. Peterson, "The Power of Now."

7. Richard Wurmbrand, *Tortured for Christ* (London: Hodder and Stoughton, 2004), 34.

4 | Meditate on the Gospel

1. Philip Yancey, "What Surprised Jesus," *Christianity Today*, September 12, 1994, accessed April 20, 2024, christianitytoday.com/ct/1994/september12/4ta088.html.

2. As cited in The Build Network Staff, "Leadership: Say It Again. And Again. (And . . .)," *Inc.com*, February 18, 2014, accessed May 30, 2024, *inc.com/the-build-network/leadership-say-it-again.html*.

3. Dr. Robert Emmons, "Pay It Forward," *Greater Good* 4 (Summer 2007): 12–15.

4. William Temple, *Nature, Man and God* (London: Macmillan, 1960), 403.

5. Quoted in Les Parrott, *High-Maintenance Relationships* (Wheaton, IL: Tyndale House, 1997), 236.

6. See Acts 27:24; 14:19–20; 23:16; 2 Corinthians 12:9; 2 Timothy 4:17.

5 | Guard the Truth

1. Steve Vogel, "Tomb Guards Stand Sentinel Through Isabel's Threatening Sweep," *Washington Post*, October 1, 2003, accessed April 30, 2024, washingtonpost.com/archive/local/2003/10/02/tomb-guards-stand-sentinel-through-isabels-threatening-sweep/87319d69-e23e-4a0a-a75c-e9a2549d1a02.

2. "Arlington Tomb Sentinels Shun Shelter," *Associated Press*, September 19, 2003, accessed at April 30, 2024, nbcnews.com/id/wbna3070198.

3. Donald Guthrie, *The Pastoral Epistles* (Grand Rapids, MI: Eerdmans, 1990), 145.

4. Barclay, *The Letters*, 151.

5. Barclay, *The Letters*, 156.

6. E. K. Simpson, *The Pastoral Epistles: The Greek Text with Introduction and Commentary* (Grand Rapids, MI: Eerdmans, 1954), 130.

7. Barclay, *The Letters*, 158.

8. As quoted in Gordon S. Jackson, *Never Scratch a Tiger with a Short Stick* (Colorado Springs, CO: NavPress, 2003), 105.

9. As quoted in "All Great Men Born Babies," *Preaching Today*, accessed May 26, 2024, preachingtoday.com/illustrations/2006/january/16286.html.

6 | Expect Tough Times

1. Hara Estroff Marano, *A Nation of Wimps: The High Cost of Invasive Parenting* (New York: Crown Archetype, 2008).

2. Warren Wiersbe, *Preaching and Teaching with Imagination* (Grand Rapids, MI: Baker Books, 1994), 24.

3. Stott, *The Message of 2 Timothy*, 56.

4. Viktor Frankl, *Man's Search for Meaning* (Boston, MA: Beacon Press, 2006), ix.

5. Quoted in Barclay, *The Letters*, 170.

6. Ortberg, *The Life You've Always Wanted*, 208.

7. For the idea of reigning with Christ, see Matthew 19:28; Luke 22:30; Romans 5:17; Revelation 3:21; 5:10; 20:4; and 22:5.

7 | Protect Your Character

1. Walter Liefeld, *1 & 2 Timothy, Titus*, The NIV Application Commentary (Grand Rapids, MI: Zondervan, 1999), 267.

2. Randy Alcorn, *The Purity Principle* (Sisters, OR: Multnomah, 2003), 45–46.

3. W. E. Vine, *An Expository Dictionary of New Testament Words* (Nashville, TN: Thomas Nelson, 1985), 73.

4. Karl Vaters, "No, I Don't Want to 'Shut Down an Atheist in 15 Seconds Flat!'" *Christianity Today*, January 24, 2018, accessed May 30, 2024, christianitytoday.com/karl-vaters/2018/january/dont-want -to-shut-down-atheist-in-15-seconds-flat.html.

5. Aaron Franco and Morgan Radford, "Ex-KKK Member Denounces Hate Groups One Year After Rallying in Charlottesville," *NBC News*, August 9, 2018, accessed May 30, 2024, nbcnews.com/ news/us-news/ex-kkk-member-denounces-hate-groups-one-year-after -rallying-n899326.

8 | Choose Wise Examples

1. John Ortberg, "Balcony People," accessed May 30, 2024, preachingtoday.com/sermons/sermons/2008/april/balconypeople. html.

2. "Practice What You Preach," December 29, 2009, accessed May 30, 2024, sermonsillustration.blogspot.com/2009/12/practice-what -you-preach.html.

3. Matthew Henry, *Matthew Henry's Commentary in One Volume* (Grand Rapids, MI: Zondervan, 1961), 1890–91.

4. "To Illustrate," *Leadership Journal* (Winter 1995): 48.

5. Barclay, *The Letters*, 195.

6. Michael Card, *The Walk* (Nashville, TN: Thomas Nelson, 2001), 109.

7. As quoted in Gordon MacDonald, *A Resilient Life* (Nashville, TN: Thomas Nelson, 2006), 229.

9 | Nourish Yourself on Scripture

1. As quoted by Dr. Albert Mohler, class lecture, Southern Baptist Theological Seminary (March 2005).

2. Norman Geisler, *To Understand the Bible Look for Jesus* (Eugene, OR: Wipf and Stock, 1979), 83.

3. John Ortberg, *The Life You've Always Wanted.*

4. This quote is often attributed to Charles Spurgeon.

5. Warren Wiersbe, *The Bible Exposition Commentary,* Vol. 2 (Wheaton, IL: Victor, 2009), 253.

6. "State of the Bible 2021: Five Key Findings," *Barna*, May 19, 2021, accessed May 30, 2024, barna.com/research/sotb-2021.

7. Rainer Maria Rilke as quoted in Eugene Peterson, *Eat This Book* (Grand Rapids, MI: Eerdmans, 2006), 4.

8. Dallas Willard, *Hearing God* (Downers Grove, IL: IVP, 2012), 212.

9. Seth Wilson, "Do You Have It in Your Heart?"

10. Donald Bullen, *A Man of One Book?* (Waynesboro, PA: Paternoster, 2007), xix.

10 | Speak God's Message

1. William Shakespeare, *Richard II*, act 2, scene 1, lines 5–6.

2. Stott, *The Message of 2 Timothy*, 107.

3. Billy Graham, *Just As I Am* (New York, NY: HarperCollins, 1997), 472–73.

4. Graham, *Just As I Am*, 473.

11 | Cultivate Real Community

1. L. F. Berkman and S. L. Syme, "Social Networks, Host Resistance, and Mortality: A Nine-Year Follow-Up Study of Alameda County Residents," *American Journal of Epidemiology* (February 1979): 186–204.

2. John Ortberg, *Everybody's Normal Till You Get to Know Them* (Grand Rapids, MI: Zondervan, 2003), 33.

3. MacDonald, *A Resilient Life*, 211.

4. Nelson Mandela, *Long Walk to Freedom* (Boston, MA: Back Bay Books, 1995), 390.

5. George S. Duncan, *The Epistle of Paul to the Galatians* (London: Hodder and Stoughton, 1934), 123.

6. Dietrich Bonhoeffer, *Life Together* (San Francisco, CA: Harper and Row, 1954), 27.

7. Stu Weber, *Locking Arms* (Sisters, OR: Multnomah, 1995), 13–14.

12 | Stay Close to Jesus

1. Stott, *The Message of 2 Timothy*, 49.

2. Stott, *The Message of 2 Timothy*, 124.

3. Quoted in Robert Smith, *Doctrine That Dances* (Nashville: B&H Publishing, 2008), 191.

4. Brother Lawrence and Frank Laubach, *Practicing His Presence* (Jacksonville, FL: SeedSowers, 1973), 10, 19.

5. As quoted in John Ortberg, *If You Want to Walk on Water, You've Got to Get Out of the Boat* (Grand Rapids: Zondervan, 2001), 165.

6. As quoted in Ortberg, *If You Want to Walk on Water*, 165.

7. Ortberg, *If You Want to Walk on Water*, 166.

8. John McRay, "Stench, Pain and Misery," *Christian History*, July 1, 1995.

9. As cited in MacDonald, *A Resilient Life*, 13–14.

About the Author

Matt Proctor has served as president of Ozark Christian College in Joplin, Missouri, since 2006. He is the author of two books, former president of the North American Christian Convention, and a past contributing editor of *Christian Standard* magazine. When he's not traveling to preach, Matt teaches children's church, tolerates the family livestock (donkey, chickens, sheep), and cheers for the St. Louis Cardinals with his wife, Katie, their six children, and their growing tribe of grandchildren.